The Three Character Classic

A Bilingual Reader of China's ABCs

三字經: 中華蒙學經典

漢英雙語讀本

The Three Character Classic

A Bilingual Reader of China's ABCs

三字經: 中華蒙學經典

漢英雙語讀本

Original Chinese Text by Wang Yinglin

Translated and Annotated by

Phebe Xu Gray

徐秀麗

HOMA & SEKEY BOOKS
PARAMUS, NEW JERSEY

Library of Congress Cataloging-in-Publication Data

880-01 Wang, Yinglin, 1223-1296.
   [880-02 San zi jing. English]
   The Three Character Classic : a bilingual reader of China's ABCs / original Chinese text by Wang Yinglin ; translated and annotated by Phebe Xu Gray. -- 1st ed.
       p. cm.
   Chinese and English, with original text in classical Chinese and its translation into both modern Chinese and English.
   Includes bibliographical references.
   ISBN 978-1-931907-71-2 (pbk.)
  1. Chinese language--Readers.   I. Gray, Phebe X., 1969- II. Title.
   PL1115.W3913 2011
   495.1'86421--dc21
                          2010039219

Published by Homa & Sekey Books
3rd Floor, North Tower
Mack-Cali Center III
140 E. Ridgewood Ave.
Paramus, NJ 07652

Tel: 201-261-8810; 800-870-HOMA
Fax: 201-261-8890; 201-384-6055
Email: info@homabooks.com
Website: www.homabooks.com

Printed in U.S.A.
1 3 5 7 9 10 8 6 4 2

To Amy, Lisa, Joseph, & Anna

美丽福华

TABLE OF CONTENTS

目录

英译《三字经》序

南京大学历史系教授 范毓周

　　《三字经》是中国古代儿童接受私塾教育的入门识字课本。在中国传统教育中，儿童是通过背诵《三字经》受到识字和知理的教育的。

　　《三字经》全文用三字一句，两字一韵的方式，以浅显的字句，阐发深刻的道理，系统叙述广为人知的历史故事，从中体现中国传统文化背景下的道德观念和人生哲理，构成一部儿童的基本识字课本和传统文化教材。《三字经》具有通俗、顺口、易记等特点，故从宋南起 700 多年来，广为流传，脍炙人口，历代都被奉为儿童教育的开蒙经典，甚至被推举为"蒙学之冠"，其原因即在于它在中国传统蒙学中兼具独特的识字功能、思想价值和文化魅力。

　　《三字经》传为南宋王应麟撰写，也有人认为是宋末区适子或明代黎贞所作，同时另有区适子所撰、黎贞增广之说。但多数学者认为应是南宋王应麟所作当是可信的。实际上，《三字经》在流传过程中，曾被许多学者进行增补和注释，因而在历史上出现过多种不同版本。

　　《三字经》在其流传过程中，还对社会许多教育领域产生过重要影响，为了便于掌握学习内容，各个领域的学者曾经先后模仿其形式编写过过许多类似作品，诸如《女三字经》、《地理三字经》、《医学三字经》、《西学三字经》、《工农三字经》、《军人三字经》、《佛教三字经》、《道教三字经》等，不一而足。

　　《三字经》作为儿童的启蒙读物，还曾广泛影响到汉族以外的其他民族，除了汉语多种版本外，还有蒙文和满文译本。近代以来，《三字经》又传布域外，先后出现英文和法文译本。其中 1990 年在新加坡出版的英文译本并被联合国教科文组织选入"儿童道德丛书"，在全世界范围内推广。由此足见它的价值和影响。

　　目前，在世界上流行多种《三字经》的英译版本，但由于《三字经》的内容广泛涉及到中国传统文化的多个领域，其中还有不

The Three Character Classic

少历史典故，而中、英文的语言并不具备严格的对应性，这些给译者带来不少困难和障碍。因而，现有的译本令人十分满意的还比较鲜见。美国李大学（Lee University）的徐秀丽博士有鉴于此，在充分研究汉语各种文本和语义的基础上，新译了这本《三字经》的英文译本。在她进行翻译过程中，曾和我鱼雁往还，做过多次讨论，故对她的译本水准略有所知。就我所知，由于译者兼有精通中、英文的坚实功底和对中国传统历史文化背景的通透了解，应当说她的译本是很成功的。这个译本的出版无疑将为《三字经》在西方世界的传布提供了可信的基础。我深信，她的工作将为联合国教科文组织推动的世界"儿童道德教育"产生不容低估的作用。故乐为之序，兼为之贺。

China's ABCs: Introducing San Zi Jing

蒙学经典：三字经

"A classic is a book that doesn't have to be written again."
—W. E. B. Dubois (1868-1963)

Introduction

San Zi Jing, *The Three Character Classic*, has been a classical Chinese literacy text since the 13th century. Although it was initially circulated in China as a primer for school children, it is more than a literacy text. Comparable to a pocket encyclopedia, it overviews Chinese history and important historical works containing the fundamentals of Confucianism, and teaches the basics of math and sciences as well as many moral lessons. Children used to recite San Zi Jing before they were able to read and write; learning San Zi Jing was the first step to becoming educated in China until the early 20th century. The book was also translated into many foreign languages, including Latin, English, French, Russian, and Japanese. It was written as an elementary Chinese textbook by one of the first Chinese professors at Cambridge University in the early 1900s. In 2009, the state-run Chinese Central Television (CCTV) produced a show on this book, which created a renewed interest among Chinese children and adults alike.

The Origin and Development of San Zi Jing

It was not accidental that *The Three Character Classic* came about in the Song dynasty, which is considered one of the most important periods in Chinese history. The Song dynasty is known for its economic development, achievements in the arts and literature, as well as for technological innovations in many areas, including the invention of printing, gun powder, and the compass. The Imperial Examinations, a system that was used to select government officials based on the meritocracy of their intellectual ability and excellence in language arts, was initiated in the Sui dynasty, about three centuries before Song, and became well established in the Song dynasty. As *The Three Character Classic* serves as a literacy primer and an introduction to the canon of works in Confucian philosophy, it was a must for the aspiring young boys to learn in order to advance in the Song society. Its significance was comparable to that of learning the alphabet in the West. It is within this background that *The Three Character Classic* emerged as a popular reader among school teachers and boys.

Although the original authorship was arguable, many attributed the work to Wang Yinglin (王应麟 1223–1296), a noted scholar in the Song dynasty. Although Wang Yinglin wrote many other literary works, he was mostly known for his work on San Zi Jing. It was said that he wrote this book to homeschool the children in his household. It is possible that the general content of San Zi Jing was already studied before Wang Yinglin officially compiled it into a book. However, due to Wang's authoritative work, San Zi Jing became the bona fide national elementary textbook throughout China.

三字經: 中華蒙學經典

In addition to Wang Yinglin, various scholars in later generations also contributed to this book. Among them were two Qing dynasty scholars Wang Xiang 王相 and He Xingsi □□思, and Zhang Taiyan 章太炎, a Chinese studies intellectual in the beginning of the Republic of China. These scholars were noted for their compilation, annotation, and publication of this book. Therefore it has served as the literacy primer in China for over 700 years.

The Three Character Classic held its paramount importance in Chinese education until the early twentieth century. The newly founded Republic of China embarked on a language reform initiative, wherein colloquial Chinese was preferred to classic literary Chinese. However, San Zi Jing was still used in the education system until 1949, when the Peoples Republic of China was founded. During the Cultural Revolution in the 1960s in mainland China, Confucianism and other classical literature were abolished as feudalistic influence. San Zi Jing disappeared from the formal educational scene for several decades. However, alongside the economic reform and development of China starting in the 1980s, San Zi Jing reappeared. It regained popularity since the 1990s. The 2009 Chinese Central Television Station's TV show on San Zi Jing made it a sensation in contemporary Chinese culture. Many parents, along with their children, started to learn San Zi Jing again, after this classic work was neglected for about three generations. On the other hand, San Zi Jing had always remained as a staple in Chinese language and culture education in the overseas Chinese community.

Content and Highlights

The content of *The Three Character Classic* can be divided into four parts. Part One introduces the importance of character education and the due responsibilities of parents, teachers, and students in the endeavor of successful learning. The emphasis of character education is based on Confucian philosophy and morals; Part Two introduces the cannon of Confucian classics and other history and philosophical works, prescribing the curriculum sequence of traditional education; Part Three overviews Chinese history by listing dynastical names, kings, and major historical events; and Part Four illustrates specific examples of hard-working individuals in history and their success stories, in order to exhort the students to study diligently, and fulfill their duty to their family and country.

Due to various revisions in different historical periods, there are many versions of San Zi Jing. While their content is about the same, the history part varies. Since the original work was done in the 13th century during the Southern Song dynasty, the original version of the overview of Chinese history stopped at the Song dynasty. Most current versions of San Zi Jing recount the history part to either the Qing dynasty, the last dynasty in China or to the Republic of China in 1911, when the imperial ruling was abolished and a republic of China was founded. Some versions also narrate the history to 1949, when the Communist Party led by Mao Zedong defeated the Nationalist Party led by Chiang Kai-shek, and established the People's Republic of China. This book adopts the original Song dynasty version, while providing three popular versions in the section of the historical description, one by the original Song dynasty author, the other two by Qing dynasty scholars Wang Xiang and He Xingsi.

In addition to many interesting stories, the highlight of San Zi Jing's work resides in its style. *The Three Character Classic* is written in a three-word-stanza or three-character-stanza poetic form. It is characterized by its simplicity as it is exceptionally easy to read, rhyme, and memorize. This style was copied in later generations as a popular style for many other subjects that are intended for popularity and memorization, including Chinese Medicine Three Character Classics; Buddhism Three Character Classics; and Filmmaking Three Character Classics. When the Olympic Games were held in Beijing, China, in 2008, the opening ceremony theme song was a variation of three-character-style song, a choice selection among many competing entries. The song became very popular in China and Chinese language learning community due to its beauty and simplicity in lyric and melody.

Influence in the West

When the Jesuit missionaries went to China in the 16th century, they all learned Chinese. It was very likely that they were familiar with San Zi Jing. Matteo Ricci, one of the most well-known Jesuits, took Li Madou as his Chinese name, with the character *dou* being a famous person (Dou Yansan) in the book of San Zi Jing. *The Three Character Classic* was introduced to the West in the 19th century. It was first translated into English by Robert Morrison, a protestant missionary to China. It was translated into French and Latin during the 19th century as well. One of the first Chinese professors at Cambridge University, Herbert Giles, who introduced the Wade-Giles Romanization system by making Chinese characters phonetically comprehensible to westerners, translated San Zi Jing into English again, and published it as an elementary Chinese textbook in 1900. Gile's original translation was republished in the U.S. in 1963. Since then, there has not been any translation and publication of this book in the United States. S.T. Phen, a scholar at Fudan University in Shanghai, published an English translation of this book in Singapore in 1989. In 2005, German scholar Friedrich Bischoff published *San Tzu Ching Explicated* in Austria. However, he only discussed the first eleven verses of San Zi Jing in his book. In addition, an on-line translation of San Zi Jing by Professor Louis Smogor from De-Pauw University (Indiana, U.S.A.) is available.

As sinology, the study of China, is a relatively new and narrow field in the West since the late 19th century and early 20th century, few westerners systematically study Chinese history, language, literature, and culture. For those who do study Chinese language, literature, and philosophy, their focus is generally on the cannon of Confucianism, Daoism, or Chinese literature. *The Three Character Classic* was often overlooked. However, a few western scholars did find San Zi Jing a useful and versatile work, and used it in their classrooms both at the undergraduate- and graduate-level courses in teaching Chinese language and culture.

Contemporary Application

Chinese commentaries of San Zi Jing had been published in mainland China from the 17th century until recent years; scholars in Taiwan, Singapore, and Hong Kong also wrote about this book. However, there are few bilingual translations (English and Chinese) of this book. This book provides a contemporary bilingual translation in Chinese and English, with special historical background information in English for Chinese language and culture learners.

As San Zi Jing reappeared as an important work in contemporary China, at a time when the popularity of learning Chinese language and culture is increasing in the West, it is high time for westerners to learn about this classic work in Chinese culture. San Zi Jing offers a unique perspective and serves as a reference to Chinese culture, and of course, it can also be used as a textbook to learn the Chinese language, and specifically, classic Chinese.

It is very beneficial for any westerners whose goal is to become proficient in the Chinese language and culture to be introduced to the moral foundations in Chinese culture as numerated in San Zi Jing, and become familiar with the stories, people, and historical events in this book. By doing so, they join in a fine tradition and the mainstream of Chinese thoughts.

On the other hand, the readers may note that San Zi Jing over emphasizes Confucianism and focuses on the importance of book learning, ignoring other schools of traditional Chinese philosophical thoughts, and neglecting the cultivation of other types of intelligence, such as kinesthetic intelligence. Modern readers will need to read critically and learn accordingly.

Special Features of This Book

This book coincides with the centennial anniversary of an important era in Chinese history: the demise of Qing Dynasty in 1911, and thus the ending of traditional classical Chinese education. This book is the first Chinese-English bilingual version book on San Zi Jing published in the U.S. since the reprinting of Giles's translation in 1963. The following are special features of this book:

1. The original text of San Zi Jing was based on one of the earliest versions in existence, written and annotated by Wang Xiang, and published in 1778.
2. There is a bilingual translation of the classic Chinese into modern Chinese and English.
3. Individual words of classic Chinese were selected and annotated with English translation.
4. A background information section is provided for each chapter to help the readers better understand Chinese culture and the context of the original text.

Conclusion

San Zi Jing, *The Three Character Classic*, has stood the test of time and space through its rich content and its beauty in simplicity in style. It is still a treat for both contemporary Chinese and Westerners to read and appreciate this classic Chinese work. Understanding San Zi Jing enables the readers to better understand Chinese culture, history, and language. Like all classics, after surviving seven centuries of time, it is likely that *The Three Character Classic* will remain in the mainstream of Chinese education and culture, not only in China, but also in the Chinese language learning community overseas for some time to come.

三字經: 中華蒙學經典

三
字
經

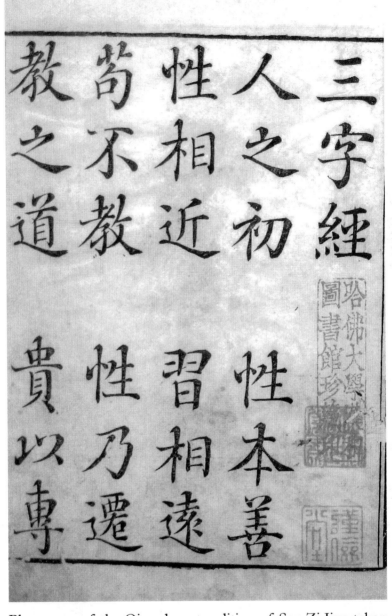

Photocopy of the Qing dynasty edition of San Zi Jing taken
at the Harvard Yenching Library Rare Books Collection

Photocopy of the Qing dynasty edition of San Zi Jing taken
at the Harvard Yenching Library Rare Books Collection

Part One

(Chpaters 1-26)

The Importance of Character Education

Chapter 1

Original Text in Simplified Characters:

rén	zhī	chū	xìng	běn	shàn
人	之	初,	性	本	善。

xìng	xiāng	jìn	xí	xiāng	yuǎn
性	相	近,	习	相	远。

Original Text in Traditional Characters:

人　　之　　初,　　性　　本　　善。
性　　相　　近,　　習　　相　　遠。

Notes:

之: a classic Chinese word equivalent to modern Chinese "的。"

初: beginning

性: nature, character, disposition

本: origin, originally

善: good

相: mutual, mutually

近: close, similar

习: practice, habits

远: far, different

Modern Chinese:

人在刚出生的时候，本性都是良好的。每个人的性情本来很相近，但是由于受各种影响，慢慢会养成相差很远的习气，性情也会变得差别很大。（因此，小孩子的可塑性很大。）

Translation:

When people were born, their moral nature was good. Their disposition was similar as well. However, due to various factors of external influence, people form different habits, which results in great differences in their dispositions.

Background information:

The opening chapter of this classic primer establishes the importance and means of character education. It argues that it is important to set a solid foundation in developmental periods of early stages in life, and there is much plasticity in the quality formation of young people. Confucian thought has been dominating Chinese culture, society, and education since the 1st century. Unlike Christianity, which considers man born with a sinful nature, Confucianism considers man to be endowed with a capacity for good  character. It attributes the evils of man to environmental factors. Therefore, men are creatures of conditioning. Confucianism puts much emphasis on moral education, warning youth to learn from good examples and shun bad examples.

Chapter 2

Original Text in Simplified Characters:

gǒu	bú	jiào	xìng	nǎi	qiān
苟	不	教，	性	乃	迁。

jiào	zhī	dào	guì	yǐ	zhuān
教	之	道，	贵	以	专。

Original Text in Traditional Characters:

苟	不	教，	性	乃	遷。
教	之	道，	貴	以	專。

Notes:

苟: if

乃: then

迁: to move, to change

道: way, road, method

贵: valuable, importance

以: with, because of

专: focus

Modern Chinese:

孩子如果不进行教育和引导，本来良好的性情也会改变；
而教导和学习的关键在于专注。（一方面教学要有目标，
另一方面要教育小孩子学会专心致志、持之以恒、始终
不懈。）

Translation:

If children are not taught properly, their innate good moral character will change. The key to teaching and learning is focus.

Background information:

Education has always been an important emphasis in Chinese culture. Education starts as early as in the womb. In traditional Chinese culture, a pregnant woman was advised to retreat to places of respite so that she could focus on cultivating her mind, body, and spirit. In addition to nutrition, she was to exercise special caution in temperament for the benefit of her fetus as well. She was to walk and sit upright, avoid unpleasant sights and noisy sounds, be moderate in speech and diet, uphold moral principles, and do good deeds in loyalties and filial piety so that her child would be born of extraordinary intellect and virtue. Even to this day, there is much emphasis and various resources for perspective mothers to teach their unborn children in music, language, and math.

While fetal education was the first stage in life, the second stage follows when children became toddlers. They were taught to use the right hand when they could feed themselves; to speak in subdued tones and to avoid yelling and throwing temper tantrums; to walk upright and properly; to bow to their elders. At this stage, their teachers were their mothers and nurses. When the children grew older, their fathers and teachers would teach them social skills and rites, music, archery, language, calligraphy, and math. In modern China, children no longer need to bow to the elders, but they still need to show respect to elders, including addressing the older playmates properly as *gege* (elder brother) or *jiejie* (elder sister). All children are taught to use their right hand in writing. They are corrected if they are left-handed.

Chapter 3

Original Text in Simplified Characters:

xī	mèng	mǔ	zé	lín	chù
昔	孟	母，	择	邻	处。

zǐ	bù	xué	duàn	jī	zhù
子	不	学，	断	机	杼。

Original Text in Traditional Characters:

昔	孟	母，	擇	鄰	處。
子	不	學，	斷	機	杼。

Notes:

昔: the past

孟母: Mengzi's mother, Mencius' mother

择: to choose

邻处: neighborhood

断: to cut off; break

机杼: a part of the loom

Modern Chinese:

古时候，孟子的母亲为了孟子的学业免受不良的影响，先后搬了三次家。孟子不好好学习时，他的母亲为了教导他，把织布机上正在织的布剪断，告诉他学习也像织布一样，不可以中途而废。

Translation:

In the past, Mencius' (Mengzi's) mother relocated three times

三字經：中華蒙學經典

to avoid bad influences in the neighborhood in order for Mencius to concentrate on study. When Mencius stopped focusing on learning, she cut the fabric she was weaving to teach him a lesson that studying is like making a garment, and a garment could not be made without consistent work.

Background information:

Mengzi was a famous Confucian philosopher and teacher who lived in the 4th century BCE. He believed men and women were born good. However, because there is evil in society and the environment, people learn to be bad. Mengzi was raised by his mother. It is said that she relocated three times to avoid perceived bad influences（孟母三迁）. They initially lived by a

断机教子

blacksmith, and Mengzi enjoyed imitating blacksmithing. Then he and his mother moved to a village where Mengzi imitated the villagers by digging graves. Finally, they settled down by a school, where Mengzi modeled the school teacher. Once, when Mengzi skipped school to play, his mother cut the fabric she was weaving and demonstrated that study needs hard work, like the making of a garment. The garment could not be finished if the weaver stopped making the fabric.

Chapter 4

Original Text in Simplified Characters:

dòu	yān	shān	yǒu	yì	fāng
窦	燕	山，	有	义	方。

jiào	wǔ	zǐ	míng	jù	yáng
教	五	子，	名	俱	扬。

Original Text in Traditional Characters:

竇	燕	山，	有	義	方。
教	五	子，	名	俱	揚。

Notes:

燕山: Mount Yan, in the northern part of China

义: righteousness, correct

方: method

俱: all

扬: to raise, to spread, to make known, to become famous

Modern Chinese:

五代时的窦禹均出生在燕山，后人称他为窦燕山，很会教育孩子。他的五个儿子长大后都很有建树，美名远扬。

Translation:

A man by the name of Dou Yujun was born in Mount Yan in the Five Dynasties period. He was referred as Dou Yanshan later. Dou was very effective in educating his children. His five sons all grew up to be successful and well-known individuals.

三字經：中華蒙學經典

Background information:

Mount Yan is near today's Beijing. In the historical record of the Song dynasty, right after the Five Dynasties period, Dou was said to be a wealthy but reckless youth. However, he repented his way and was rewarded with five sons later. He was devoted to good deeds in the community and the education of his sons. Dou was especially known for being strict with his children. All of them passed the imperial examination and

窦氏五龙

became civil servants in the government. A popular Chinese saying, *wu zi deng ke*, 五子登科, literally meaning, five children passing Imperial Examinations, is a popular saying that originated from Dou's story. People used Dou Yanshan as an example to wish parents and their children for a prosperous future. Matteo Ricci, the renowned Jesuit missionary who went to China in the 16th century and became well versed in Chinese language, literature, and culture, was so impressed with the story of Dou that he took Dou's name for his Chinese name, Li Ma Dou （利玛窦）.

Chapter 5

Original Text in Simplified Characters:

yǎng	bú	jiào	fù	zhī	guò
养	不	教，	父	之	过。
jiào	bù	yán	shī	zhī	duò
教	不	严，	师	之	惰。

Original Text in Traditional Characters:

養	不	教，	父	之	過。
教	不	嚴，	師	之	惰。

Notes:

养: to raise children, to support

过: mistake, fault

严: strict, stern

惰: lazy, laziness

Modern Chinese:

对于孩子，只养活而不教育，是做父亲的过错。同样，老师教育学生如不认真严格，就是懒惰的行为。

Translation:

If a father merely raises his children but neglects their education, he is to be at fault. Likewise, if a teacher only instructs the students, yet is negligent in disciplining them, then the teacher is lazy.

三字經: 中華蒙學經典

Background information:

In Chinese education, teachers are expected to be strict. It is said that "strict teachers produce extraordinary students," *yan shi chu gao tu*, 严师出高徒。 Teachers' authority over students is similar to that of parents over children; they are to be obeyed and respected by the students. In Chinese language, teacher can also be called *shi fu* 师父, or *shi ye* 师爷, which literally means "teacher-father" or "teacher-grandfather." On the other hand, a father is entrusted with the responsibility of educating and disciplining his children at home. The traditional Chinese fam-

ily is highly hierarchical with the father as the head of the household. A father has much authority and responsibility. If children turn out to be wayward bound, people tend to blame the father rather than the mother.

Chapter 6

Original Text in Simplified Characters:

zǐ	bù	xué	fēi	suǒ	yí
子	不	学，	非	所	宜。

yòu	bù	xué	lǎo	hé	wéi
幼	不	学，	老	何	为？

Original Text in Traditional Characters:

子	不	學，	非	所	宜。
幼	不	學，	老	何	為？

Notes:

子: child

非: not

宜: proper, appropriate

幼: young

何: what

为: to do, to become

Modern Chinese:

孩子不接受教育，是不妥当的。一个人如果小时候不努力学习，那么到老的时候还会有什么成就和作为呢？

Translation:

If a child does not apply himself in learning, it is indeed inappropriate. If a person does not learn at youth, what can he accomplish in old age?

三字經: 中華蒙學經典

Background information:

In Chinese culture, precociousness is encouraged in children. All children are expected to study hard to prepare for their future. While there is an overemphasis on learning, there is less emphasis on "letting the children be children," not allowing children to play and enjoy themselves. There is a general sense of urgency among parents and teachers in warning children about how precious their time is. Even though the idea of critical period theory is not prevalent in its scientific form among lay Chinese, its application is accepted by Chinese in practice. Critical period theory notes that there is a biological period, in which there is a heightened sensitivity that allows children to learn, this period is sometimes referred to as the window of opportunity in learning. Parents and teachers admonish youth to fully take advantage of the learning opportunity in this period. A Chinese proverb says that if a person does not strive hard to learn in his youth, he will only have regrets left in old age, *shao xiao bu nu li, lao da tu shang bei* (少小不努力，老大徒伤悲).

While a young man is expected to study hard, there are prescribed expectations for other age periods as well. Although they were originated with Confucius' personal life, the expectations were used to apply to people in general. At 15, a person should engage in learning; at 30, one is to establish himself in family and career; at 40, one is to have no doubt in life; at 50, one is to know the will of God; at 60, one is to be tolerant; at 70, one can do whatever his heart tells him to do, and he will not violate any rules (十有五而志于学，三十而立，四十而不惑，五十而知天命，六十而耳顺，七十而从心所欲，不逾矩). Even though not everyone abides by these expectations, many regard them as duties to be fulfilled in life and try to measure up to these standards.

Chapter 7

Original Text in Simplified Characters:

yù	bù	zhuó	bù	chéng	qì
玉	不	琢，	不	成	器。
rén	bù	xué	bù	zhī	yì
人	不	学，	不	知	义。

Original Text in Traditional Characters:

玉	不	琢，	不	成	器。
人	不	學，	不	知	義。

Notes:

玉: jade

琢: to polish

成: to become, to accomplish

器: vessel, utensil

义: duty, righteousness

Modern Chinese:

一块玉石如果不经过雕琢，就不会成为精美的玉器；同样，一个人如果不学习，就不会懂得做人处事的道理。

Translation:

A jade stone will not become a useful vessel if it is not processed through various stages of polishing and carving. In the same way, a person will not understand how to live a righteous life if he does not apply himself in learning.

Background information:

Jade stonework is a unique aspect of ancient Chinese culture. Jade artifacts were discovered at some of the earliest archeological sites. Jade was made into jewelry, ornaments, tools, music instruments, utensils, and sacrificial vessels. Confucius compared the property of jade to the quality of gentlemen. Jade symbolizes beauty, purity, modesty, perfection, righteousness, and inner virtue. An ancient gentleman was to wear jade all the time to remind himself of the quality of jade and the virtue of a gentleman. The process of polishing and carving jade is a special craft in China. Since jade is a natural stone, each jade jewelry piece is a unique object; no two jade pieces are alike. It is said that there may be a price for gold, but as for jade, it is priceless (*huang jin you jia yu wu jia* 黄金有价玉无价).

加工玉器图

Chapter 8

Original Text in Simplified Characters:

wéi	rén	zǐ	fāng	shào	shí
为	人	子，	方	少	时。

qīn	shī	yǒu	xí	lǐ	yí
亲	师	友，	习	礼	仪。

Original Text in Traditional Characters:

為	人	子，	方	少	時。
親	師	友，	習	禮	儀。

Notes:

为: to be

子: child, student

方: at the time, just

少时: youthful time, young time

亲: to be close to, to become intimate

礼仪: etiquette, protocol

Modern Chinese:

作为孩儿和学生，一个人应该从小就去结交良师益友，探究学习做人的礼仪。

Translation:

As a child and student, a young person should seek productive fellowship with teachers and friends, so as to learn proper etiquette and decorum to behave well in all areas of life.

三字經: 中華蒙學經典

Background information:

This chapter advises on the importance of dynamic fellowship in a person's life. People should seek good teachers for mentors, and to find good friends to be influenced by. Good teachers and positive friends will facilitate in productive character formation. In traditional China, teachers may not accept anyone who wants to be their students. Devoted students must prove themselves worthy to be accepted as disciples through sincerity and determination. Once accepted, the students become "family" members of the teacher as disciples.

When the students join in true fellowship with teachers and friends, they are to learn proper ways in behavior as well. To learn proper ways to conduct oneself is more important than having mere knowledge. Unlike animals, people are obligated to moral duties, decorum, and proprieties in a civilized society.

孟僖子与南宫敬叔
向孔子学礼

Chapter 9

Original Text in Simplified Characters:

xiāng	jiǔ	líng	néng	wēn	xí
香	九	龄，	能	温	席。
xiào	yú	qīn	suǒ	dāng	zhí
孝	于	亲，	所	当	执。

Original Text in Traditional Characters:

香	九	齡，	能	溫	席。
孝	于	親，	所	當	執。

Notes:

龄: age

温: to warm up

亲: parents

席: mat

孝: filial piety

所: therefore

当: ought to, should

执: to hold, to carry out, to observe

Modern Chinese:

东汉有一个叫黄香的孩子，九岁的时候就懂得孝敬父母。冬天很冷的时候，他用自己的身体先把床被温暖后再请父母睡觉。孝敬父母是每个人义不容辞的责任。

三字經: 中華蒙學經典

Translation:

There was a boy named Huan Xiang in the Eastern Han dynasty. When he was only nine years old, as it was very cold in the wintertime, Huang Xiang would first warm up the blanket with his body heat, and then invite his parents to sleep. People should have filial piety toward their parents. This is everyone's duty and responsibility.

Background information:

Filial piety stories are passed down through generations. Filial means love to be befitting a son or daughter; filial piety means love and devotion to parents and elders. A classic Chinese book was called *Twenty-four Filial Piety*, 二十四孝, recording twenty four filial piety stories, teaching children to be filial to their parents. The story of Huang Xiang is one of the stories. It was also said that Huang Xiang would cool the bed with a fan for his parents in the summer, and warm up the bed for them with his body heat in winter. Other stories tell about different ways that both children and adults demonstrate filial piety to their parents. For example, one story tells about a child known for his intelligence. One time he was invited to visit an official's house, and he was given some oranges to eat. Upon leaving, he sneaked an orange in his sleeves. When confronted, the child said he did so because he knew his mother liked oranges very much and he wanted to bring one to his mother.

Another story tells of a boy who let the mosquitoes bite him on purpose in his house without chasing them away in the summer, and the reason for him in doing so was that he would rather the mosquitoes bite him than his parents. Another filial piety story tells about a son who used to carry rice for his parents from faraway places when he was poor. Later on, he became an official and did not need to carry rice by himself anymore. However, after his parents passed away, he

黄香为父亲扇枕温席

lamented the fact that even if he wanted to carry the rice once again for his parents, he no longer had the opportunity to do so. He warned others to take advantage of the time they had with their parents.

Chapter 10

Original Text in Simplified Characters:

róng	sì	suì	néng	ràng	lí
融	四	岁，	能	让	梨。

dì	yú	zhǎng	yí	xiān	zhī
弟	于	长，	宜	先	知。

Original Text in Traditional Characters:

融	四	歲，	能	讓	梨。
弟	于	長，	宜	先	知。

Notes:

能: can, be capable of

让: to give in, to yield

长: the elders

宜: should, ought

Modern Chinese:

东汉有一个叫孔融的小孩，四岁时就知道尊敬兄长，把大的梨子让给哥哥，自己吃小的。弟弟要尊敬兄长的道理从小就应该知道。

Translation:

There was a child by the name of Kong Rong in the Eastern Han period. When he was four years old, he offered the bigger and choice pears to his brothers, and reserved the smaller one for himself when they had to share some pears on an occasion. This is an example of the principle regarding a younger brother respecting the elder brother. Everyone should know this principle at childhood.

Background information:

Kong Rong (153-208) was a direct descendant of Confucius, the most famous Chinese philosopher. Kong Rong was one among seven siblings, five of his brothers were older, and one of them was younger. He was an extremely bright child. When he gave the larger pears to his brothers, he was asked why he did so. Kong Rong replied, "I am younger than my elder brothers. Therefore, I ought to respect them, and let them have the larger pears. On the other hand, I am older than my younger brother. Therefore, I ought to take care of him, and let him have a larger one."

Confucius' thought emphasized filial piety, while a younger person is to love and respect for the parents and older siblings in the family, parents and elder siblings were to love and take care of the younger ones. This principle also applies to authority and older people in general. Even though Kong Rong was an accomplished literary scholar later in life, he was most well known for his good manners toward his elder brothers as a child.

三字經: 中華蒙學經典

Chapter 11

Original Text in Simplified Characters:

shǒu	xiào	dì	cì	jiàn	wén
首	孝	弟，	次	见	闻。

zhī	mǒu	shù	shí	mǒu	wén
知	某	数，	识	某	文。

Original Text in Traditional Characters:

首	孝	弟，	次	見	聞。
知	某	數，	識	某	文。

Notes:

首: foremost, primarily, first

弟: same as 悌，fraternal love

次: secondarily, second

见闻: knowledge, what one sees and hears

某: certain, some

Modern Chinese:

做人最重要的是孝敬父母，尊重师长，其次才是学习知识，增长见识，既要学习数理，也要学习语文，力求文理兼优。

Translation:

The first and foremost important task in a person's life is to fulfill filial piety towards parents and elders. Secondarily, he is to acquire knowledge through various channels. He should know math and sciences, as well as language arts, in order to be a well-rounded person.

Background information:

This chapter establishes the priority of a person's life. It places filial piety on the top of the agenda. Respecting parents and elders is more important than the mere acquisition of knowledge. This chapter also proposes a well-rounded education curriculum for the students. In addition to books, the students are advised to learn from "seeing and hearing," meaning that they should gain knowledge from extra-curriculum activities. The stu-

dents ought to know subjects in both sciences and liberal arts. It is interesting that this recommendation places sciences before language arts, indicating that children should learn numbers and concepts of mathematics before learning how to read.

Chapter 12

Original Text in Simplified Characters:

yī	ér	shí	shí	ér	bǎi
一	而	十，	十	而	百。

bǎi	ér	qiān	qiān	ér	wàn
百	而	千，	千	而	万。

Original Text in Traditional Characters:

一	而	十，	十	而	百。
百	而	千，	千	而	萬。

Notes:

而: and, then

百: hundred

千: thousand

万: ten thousand

Modern Chinese:

从一到十，从十到百；百以后的数量单位是千，千以后的数量单位是万。

Translation:

In counting numbers, it goes from one to ten, then from ten to a hundred; the unit after hundred is thousand, and the unit after thousand is ten thousand.

Background information:

China was very advanced in mathematics in ancient times. In the book *The Genius of China: 3,000 Years of Science, Discovery and Invention* written by Robert K. G. Temple (Simon and Schuster, 1986), which was a condensed version of Joseph Needham's monumental scholarly work *History and Science of Chinese civilization*, it notes that the decimal place system, or base 10 system, was used as early as the Shang dynasty (1766-1122 BCE), more than two thousand years earlier than that being used in the West. Correspondingly, when translating Chinese mathematic terminologies, there is *ge* for ones, *shi* for tens, *bai* for hundreds, *qian* for thousands, *wan* for ten thousands, and *baiwan* for million.

In the Zhou dynasty (1122-256 BCE), a Chinese gentleman was expected to master six arts. Besides etiquette, music, archery, charioting, and calligraphy, mathematic proficiency was one of the six fundamental skills required for a learned person.

Chapter 13

Original Text in Simplified Characters:

sān	cái	zhě	tiān	dì	rén
三	才	者,	天	地	人。
sān	guāng	zhě	rì	yuè	xīng
三	光	者,	日	月	星。

Original Text in Traditional Characters:

三	才	者,	天	地	人。
三	光	者,	日	月	星。

三字經: 中華蒙學經典

Notes:

才: force, fundamental power

者: ones

光: light

Modern Chinese:

古代称"天"、"地"和"人"为"三才"，认为这是构成宇宙三种要素。又把"太阳"、"月亮"和"星辰"叫作"三光"，因为它们是天空中发出光辉的天体。

Translation:

There are three most fundamental elements in the universe: they are heaven, earth, and man. There are three luminary objects: they are sun, moon, and stars.

Background information:

The consideration of the three forces: the energy of heaven, earth, and man is vital in matters big and small in Chinese culture. They are also referred to as three essential elements for success. Heaven, *tian shi* 天时, refers to factors in timing, weather, opportunity, and circumstances beyond control; earth, *di li* 地利, refers to factors in geography, location, environment, and the physical facilities in a given situation; man, *ren he* 人和, refers to factors in interpersonal relationships. In the book *The Art of War*, 孙子兵法, the 6th century BCE Chinese master military strategist Sun Zi 孙子 noted that if a battle was won without harmony in all three factors of heaven, earth, and man, the battle was lost indeed. The philosopher Mencius maintained that to have the advantage of heaven is not as good as having the advantage of earth; to have the advantage of earth is not as good as having the advantage of man. In another word, Mencius argued that it is more important to have better interpersonal relationships in all circumstances (*Tian shi bu ru di li, di li bu ru ren he*) 天时不如地利，地利不如人和. In conducting business, a wise Chinese person would evaluate the situation in each of the three elements of heaven, earth, and man to assess how they may contribute to one's ultimate success.

The Ancient Chinese were very advanced in astronomy, too. Among many achievements, the Chinese lunar calendar, celestial globe, and seismograph were a few examples of Chinese inventions.

Chapter 14

Original Text in Simplified Characters:

sān	gāng	zhě	jūn	chén	yì
三	纲	者，	君	臣	义。
fù	zǐ	qīn	fū	fù	shùn
父	子	亲，	夫	妇	顺。

Original Text in Traditional Characters:

三	綱	者，	君	臣	義。
父	子	親，	夫	婦	順。

Notes:

纲: guiding principle

君臣: king/emperor and subject; prince and minister

义: duty, obligation, righteousness

父子: father and son

亲: to love

夫妇: husband and wife

顺: agreeable, harmonious

Modern Chinese:

古时候，做人有三项重要原则，即君主和臣属之间要遵循道义，父亲和儿子之间要重视亲情，丈夫和妻子之间要温顺和睦。

Translation:

In traditional Chinese culture, there are three very important principles that guide interpersonal relationships that one must obey. There should be righteousness and justice between a king/emperor and his ministers; love and affection between father and son; and gentleness and harmony between husband and wife.

Background information:

A famous Chinese national hero, Yue Fei 岳飞, has been admired for his righteousness and loyalty to his country and the emperor for centuries. Yue Fei was a general in the Song dynasty, who fought bravely against the invading enemy from the North. It was said that Yue Fei's mother tattooed four characters "Uttermost Loyalty for Country 精忠报国" on his back to serve as a reminder of his duty to his country. Yue Fei was extraordinarily courageous and most capable in maneuvering his army against the enemy. Yue's devotion to righteousness and loyalty to the emperor and his country made him a national hero. There are many popular stories about Yue Fei.

Chapter 15

Original Text in Simplified Characters:

yuē	chūn	xià	yuē	qiū	dōng
曰	春	夏,	曰	秋	冬。

cǐ	sì	shí	yùn	bù	qióng
此	四	时,	运	不	穷。

Original Text in Traditional Characters:

曰	春	夏,	曰	秋	冬。
此	四	時,	運	不	窮。

Notes:

曰: to say, to speak

春夏秋冬: spring, summer, fall, winter

此: this, these

四时: four seasons

运: to carry, to revolve, to cycle

不穷: no end; endlessly

Modern Chinese:

一年的四个季节是春、夏、秋、冬。这四个季节循环运转，没有尽头。

Translation:

There are four seasons in a year: spring, summer, fall, and winter. These four seasons operate in an endless cyclical fashion.

Background information:

In ancient Chinese astronomy, it was observed that the cycling of four seasons is a result of the rotating of the Big Dipper in the sky. In spring, the handle of the Bigger Dipper points east, in summer, it points south; in autumn, the handle points west; and in winter, the handle points north. The four seasons also correspond to stages in human development, whereas spring is childhood, summer is youth, autumn is adulthood, and winter is old age. The four seasons have much significance in traditional Chinese medicine as well. If one has a sickness related to the winter season, as for example, asthma, then it is best treated in the summer. In literature, spring is often associated with sensuality, while autumn is associated with loneliness. The four seasons is a common theme depicted in traditional Chinese painting.

Chapter 16

Original Text in Simplified Characters:

yuē	nán	běi	yuē	xī	dōng
曰	南	北，	曰	西	东。
cǐ	sì	fāng	yìng	hū	zhōng
此	四	方，	应	乎	中。

Original Text in Traditional Characters:

曰	南	北，	曰	西	東。
此	四	方，	應	乎	中。

Notes:
四方: four directions

南北西东: south, north, west, east

应乎: to respond to

Modern Chinese:

宇宙中的四个方位是东、南、西、北。这四个方位都与中央相对应。（随着中央点的移动，东南西北的方向也会变动。方位是相对而论的。）

Translation:

The four directions in the universe are north, south, east, and west. These four directions correspond to the center in the middle of China.

Background information:

The compass is one of many inventions by the Chinese people. The south-pointing compass in ancient China was originally used in fengshui traditions to assess building construction. Zheng He 郑和, a Muslim general in the Ming dynasty, with the aid of a compass, was very successful in his famous maritime adventures. He took seven voyages between 1405 and 1433, during which he commanded the Treasure Boat visiting many southeastern nations, and went as far as West Africa.

Cartography was also an advanced science in ancient China. China has one of the earliest maps made in the world. It was a copper engraving map containing the layout of the burial sites of a royal family in Hebei province, on which proper directions and scales were clearly labeled.

In naming the four directions, Chinese list east, south, west, and north in a clockwise direction. In the original pictograph, the character for the word "east" 东 was made of a son rising over a tree, symbolizing the direction of the east;

and the word "west" 西 was depicted as a bird resting on its nest ready for the evening, as the sun sets in the west.

Chapter 17

Original Text in Simplified Characters:

yuē	shuǐ	huǒ	mù	jīn	tǔ
曰	水	火，	木	金	土。

cǐ	wǔ	xíng	běn	hū	shù
此	五	行，	本	乎	数。

Original Text in Traditional Characters:

曰	水	火，	木	金	土。
此	五	行，	本	乎	數。

Notes:

水火木金土: water, fire, wood, metal, earth

五行: five elements

本乎: to have origin in; to be based on

数: numbers, math

Modern Chinese:

金、木、水、火、土是构成宇宙的基本元素，被称为"五行"。它们遵循相生相克的数理关系存在于宇宙万物之中。

Translation:

Water, fire, wood, metal, and earth are the five basic elements in the universe. They are referred to as the "Five Elements." These five elements operate in intricate relationships in every aspect of the universe.

Background information:

In Chinese fengshui culture, the Five Elements correspond to the four seasons and four directions. Wood corresponds to east and spring; fire corresponds to south and summer; metal corresponds to west and fall; water corresponds to north and winter; and earth corresponds to the center. There are productive cycles and destructive cycles, called *xiang sheng xiang ke* 相生相克. The productive cycles are thus: wood feeds fire; fire produces earth; earth bears metal; metal bears water; and water nourishes wood. The destructive cycles are: wood blocks water; water rusts metal; metal breaks up earth; earth quenches fire; and fire burns wood. These five basic elements are in all matters in the universe. Therefore, if they form a productive cycle, there will be harmony and prosperity; if the cycle is destructive, there will be chaos and ill fortune.

In addition, the Five Elements also correspond to planets, climates, body parts, colors, senses, and emotions. For example, wood is related to Jupiter, its color is green, the climate associated with wood is windy, the corresponding vital organ is liver, its external corresponding body parts are eyes, its matching sense is sight, and the analogous emotion is anger. In ancient China, match-makers compare the birth dates (*ba zi* 八字) of the prospective couple to see whether they are productive or destructive to each other. Chinese medicine also utilizes the theory of the Five Elements in diagnostic and treatment of ailments.

Chapter 18

Original Text in Simplified Characters:

yuē	rén	yì	lǐ	zhì	xìn
曰	仁	义,	礼	智	信。

cǐ	wǔ	cháng	bù	róng	wèn
此	五	常,	不	容	紊。

Original Text in Traditional Characters:

曰	仁	義,	禮	智	信。
此	五	常,	不	容	紊。

Notes:

仁: benevolence, love

义: duty, righteousness

礼: rites, propriety, etiquette, protocol

智: wisdom

信: truth, trustworthiness

五常: five virtues, five constants, five invariables

容: to tolerate, to allow, to permit

紊: confusion, disorder

Modern Chinese:

君子为人必须遵行五种基本品质，就是仁、义、礼、智、信。仁是爱人，对人有爱心；义是道义，为人应当恪守的道德和义务；礼是礼仪，待人处事的礼节和态度；智是理智，做事要有足够的理性和智慧；信是诚信，处世待人应该讲求诚恳和信用。(这五种品质在任何情形下都要恪守。)

Translation:

There are five essential virtues a gentleman ought to possess at all times in his conduct: offering love to fellow human beings, duty to others, propriety in social protocols, wisdom in thoughts and deeds, and truth in all endeavors.

Background information:

The five virtues of love, duty, propriety, wisdom, and truth are the most fundamental tenants in Confucian thoughts. Confucianism strives for maintaining order in families and society to avoid chaos. Therefore, it is essential to establish rules of conduct in interpersonal relationships to regulate behaviors and ensure order and harmony. Because families are close-knit, and traditional Chinese societies are relatively populous, it is even more important for people to adhere to moral laws to ensure peaceful living in this kind of setting.

三字經：中華蒙學經典

Chapter 19

Original Text in Simplified Characters:

dào	liáng	shú	mài	shǔ	jì
稻	粱	菽,	麦	黍	稷。

cǐ	liù	gǔ	rén	suǒ	shí
此	六	谷,	人	所	食。

Original Text in Traditional Characters:

稻　　粱　　菽,　　麦　　黍　　稷。
此　　六　　谷,　　人　　所　　食。

Notes:

稻: rice

粱: sorghum

菽: beans

麦: wheat

黍: corn

稷: millet

谷: grain

食: to eat

Modern Chinese:

稻米、高粱、豆子、小麦、玉米和小米是人类食用的六
种基本食粮。

Translation:

Rice, sorghum, beans, wheat, corn, and millet are six major varieties of grains in people's diet.

Background information:

In a Chinese diet, grains are considered *fan* 饭, which means the main dish or staple food, while meat and vegetables are considered *cai* 菜, which means side dish or non-staple food. It is customary for Chinese to eat more grains than meat and vegetables at any given meal. For breakfast and dinner, many Chinese eat porridges made of grains. Lunch is the main meal for most Chinese. While northern Chinese eat more noodles and other wheat products, a southern Chinese diet consists of more rice and rice products.

China has been an agricultural society since ancient times. Grain cultivation and grain-related products and activities are very important in Chinese culture. Grain fermentation has been a tradition in Chinese wine culture since ancient times. In archeological findings, many bronze wine vessels were uncovered. These vessels had intricate designs and some of them were decorated with entertainment motifs. These vessels indicate that the ancient Chinese had a rich wine culture.

Chapter 20

Original Text in Simplified Characters:

mǎ	niú	yáng	jī	quǎn	shǐ
马	牛	羊,	鸡	犬	豕。
cǐ	liù	chù	rén	suǒ	sì
此	六	畜,	人	所	饲。

三字經: 中華蒙學經典

Original Text in Traditional Characters:

馬　　牛　　羊，　　鷄　　犬　　豕。
此　　六　　畜，　　人　　所　　飼。

Notes:

犬: dog

豕: pig

畜: livestock, domestic animal

饲: to raise animal

Modern Chinese:

马、牛、羊、鸡、狗和猪，这六种动物是人们饲养的主
要家畜。

Translation:

There are six major types of domesticated animals. They are
horse, cow, sheep, chicken, dog, and pig.

Background information:

Family is an important concept in Chinese culture. The pictograph for family is *jia* 家，which consists of a roof (cover on
top) and a pig (in the bottom), as a pig has more litters at a
single birth than other domesticated animals. The purpose of
family is to produce offspring and continue the ancestral line.
Pork is also the most popular form of meat among Han Chinese people.

三字經: 中華蒙學經典

Chapter 21

Original Text in Simplified Characters:

yuē	xǐ	nù	yuē	āi	jù
曰	喜	怒，	曰	哀	惧。

ài	wù	yù	qī	qíng	jù
爱	恶	欲，	七	情	具。

Original Text in Traditional Characters:

曰	喜	怒，	曰	哀	懼。
愛	惡	欲，	七	情	具。

Notes:

喜: happiness

怒: anger

哀: sadness

惧: fear

欲: desire

爱: love

恶: hatred

七情: seven emotions

具: to have, to possess

Modern Chinese:

高兴、愤怒、忧伤、害怕、喜爱、憎恨和欲念，是每个人都具有的七种感情。

Translation:

Happiness, anger, sadness, fear, love, hatred, and desire are seven kinds of emotions pertaining to every human being.

Background information:

In Chinese medicine, emotions correspond to major vital organs. Happiness is related to heart; anger is related to liver; sadness to lungs; and fear to kidney. Although it is natural for everyone to have these emotions, a gentleman in Chinese culture is to keep his composure at all times without showing extreme emotions. The word "love" is commonly reserved for romantic love in Chinese culture. Parents seldom tell their children they "love" them. Instead, they may say they are pleased with them or they are happy with them. Friends may say they like each other instead of love each other.

Chapter 22

Original Text in Simplified Characters:

páo	tǔ	gé	mù	shí	jīn
匏	土	革,	木	石	金。
sī	yǔ	zhú	nǎi	bā	yīn
丝	与	竹,	乃	八	音。

Original Text in Traditional Characters:

匏	土	革,	木	石	金。
絲	與	竹,	乃	八	音。

三字經: 中華蒙學經典

Notes:

匏: gourd

革: leather

丝: silk

竹: bamboo

八音: eight sounds, music

Modern Chinese:

中国传统的乐器是由八种不同的材料做成的，称为"八音"。它们是匏瓜做成的笙，陶土做成的埙，皮革做成的鼓，木头做成的木鱼、梆子等，玉石做成的磬，金属材料做成的钟等，丝弦做成的琴、筝和竹器做的笛、箫。

Translation:

Traditional Chinese musical instruments are made of eight different kinds of materials. They are called "Eight Sounds." Gourd makes *sheng*, a wind instrument; clay makes *xun*, a wind instrument; animal skin makes drum; wood makes wood fish and *bang zi*, two kinds of percussion instruments; jade makes *qing*, a percussion instrument; metal makes bells; silk makes the strings of *qin* (zither); and bamboo makes a flute.

Background information:

Ancient Chinese music was often used at religious and sacrificial ceremonies. Confucius noted that the purpose for music was to cultivate a person's character rather than for entertainment. A learned person should excel in playing music and chess, calligraphy, and painting. *Gu qin* (ancient zither), is the oldest musical instrument in Chinese culture. Its strings are made of silk. People may find out who their kindred spirits are by playing their favorite music on *gu qin* and see who enjoys the same kind of music. A popular *gu qin* music is called "high mountains and flowing water 高山流水." This phrase also symbolizes friendship.

Chapter 23

Original Text in Simplified Characters:

gāo	zēng	zǔ	fù	ér	shēn
高	曾	祖，	父	而	身。

shēn	ér	zǐ	zǐ	ér	sūn
身	而	子，	子	而	孙。

Original Text in Traditional Characters:

高	曾	祖，	父	而	身。
身	而	子，	子	而	孫。

Notes:

高: great great grandfather

曾: great grandfather

祖: grandfather

身: self

子: son   孙: grandson

Modern Chinese:

家族的辈份关系是这样的：以我为自身，上有四代，他们是父亲、祖父、曾祖父、高祖父；自身之下则有儿子和孙子。

三字經：中華蒙學經典

Translation:

In family relations, there are four generations older than oneself. They are one's father, grandfather, great grandfather, and great great grandfather. There are two generations younger than oneself: sons and grandsons.

Background information:

In traditional Chinese settings, families are close-knit. Chinese kinship terms are very complicated. As multigenerational family members often dwell together, it is important to designate proper titles to each person according to their generational status. Chinese family structure is patriarchal and hierarchical. Older men in the family enjoy higher status than younger men and females.

明代一郑姓大家族七世同居，有一千多人，
时称"天下第一家"

Chapter 24

Original Text in Simplified Characters:

zì	zǐ	sūn	zhì	xuán	zēng
自	子	孙,	至	玄	曾。

nǎi	jiǔ	zú	rén	zhī	lún
乃	九	族,	人	之	伦。

Original Text in Traditional Characters:

自	子	孫,	至	玄	曾。
乃	九	族,	人	之	倫。

Notes:

玄: great great grandson

曾: great grandson

九族: nine generations

伦: relationship

Modern Chinese:

中国的家庭关系又有"九族"一称。就是"我"和上面的四代、下面的四代。上面是父亲、祖父、曾祖父和高祖父。下面是儿子、孙子、曾孙和玄孙。（这四代为直系亲属，这九族之间有着尊卑和老幼的关系。）

Translation:

In China, the direct family is composed of oneself, sons, grandsons, and great grandsons. There is also the relationship of "nine generations," which is the four generations older than oneself, and four generations younger than oneself.

三字經: 中華蒙學經典

Background information:

The nine generations in Chinese family relationships are hierarchical. In ancient times, if one person in the family committed a crime, his entire family clan, including up to three, five or even nine generations, may be punished. The purpose of this punishment is that none in the family would be left to commit revenge later.

Traditional Chinese names consist of three characters: the family name, a generation name, and the first name. Generation names are used by siblings and cousins of the same generation. Many families keep record of family trees. One of the most well-kept family trees is that of the Confucius family, which, to this day, has over 80 generations with over one million descendents in China and overseas.

Chapter 25

Original Text in Simplified Characters:

fù	zǐ	ēn	fū	fù	cóng
父	子	恩，	夫	妇	从。

xiōng	zé	yǒu	dì	zé	gōng
兄	则	友，	弟	则	恭。

Original Text in Traditional Characters:

父　子　恩，　夫　婦　從。
兄　則　友，　弟　則　恭。

Notes:

恩: kindness, affection

从: obedience, harmony

则: to be

友: friendly

恭: respectful

Modern Chinese:

父亲要爱孩子，孩子要孝敬父亲；丈夫要善待妻子，妻子也要顺从丈夫。兄长要对弟弟关怀友爱，弟弟对兄长则要尊重恭敬。

Translation:

Fathers should love their children, and children should respect their fathers; husbands should be kind to their wives, and wives should obey their husbands; elder brothers should befriend their younger brothers, and younger brothers should respect older brothers.

Background information:

While there are many stories about how fathers love their sons and how brothers befriend each other in Chinese culture, some stories also teach lessons about how wives love their husbands. One of the stories is called "raising the tray to her eyebrow (*ju an qi mei* 举案齐眉)." It was about Liang Hong, a poor but virtuous scholar, and Meng Guang, his plain yet obedient wife in the Eastern Han dynasty. In this story, Meng gave up her life in the village and chose to live a hermit life with her husband when he requested so. She learned to be self-sufficient in making clothes and grew food. At a later time, her husband had to work for a rich man. Whenever he came back from work, Meng would serve the food to him, kneeling down, and raising the tray to her eyebrow, not looking at him to show respect. Liang was very kind to his wife too, treating her as polite as one did to a guest. The rich man was very touched by the harmonious relationship between the couple, and realized that they were learned people. He did not ask Liang to work for him anymore but rather, let him engage in scholarly work.

Chapter 26

Original Text in Simplified Characters:

zháng	yòu	xù	yǒu	yǔ	péng
长	幼	序，	友	与	朋。
jūn	zé	jìng	chén	zé	zhōng
君	则	敬，	臣	则	忠。
cǐ	shí	yì	rén	suǒ	tóng
此	十	义，	人	所	同。

Original Text in Traditional Characters:

長	幼	序，	友	與	朋。
君	則	敬，	臣	則	忠。
此	十	義，	人	所	同。

Notes:

序: to have order

敬: respectful

忠: loyal

十义: ten duties

Modern Chinese:

长辈和晚辈之间要有尊卑的次序。朋友之间要有良善和
信用，君主要敬重大臣，大臣要忠诚于君主。父慈子孝，
夫唱妇随，兄爱弟恭，君敬臣忠，朋友间要相互有情有
意，这是每个人都要遵守的十种道义。

Translation:

In addition to the proper relationships among fathers and
sons, husband and wife, friends, elders and younger generations, there should be proper duties of morality and justice
among the king and his subjects. Everyone should be obliged
to these ten moral duties. There should be a hierarchical order
of respect between the elder and the young; there should be
kindness and truth between friends; the king should respect
his ministers and subjects, and they should be loyal to their
king.

Background information:

To uphold friendship is one of the ten duties that people
should have. In Chinese culture, friendship is always a cele-
brated subject. Good friends sometimes have special ceremonies to take oaths to become "blood brothers, *jie bai xiong di*
结拜兄弟." They vow to help and defend each other in times
of need as brothers would do in the family.

Part Two

(Chpaters 27-44)

The Cannon of Confucian Classics

Chapter 27

Original Text in Simplified Characters:

fán	xùn	méng	xū	jiǎng	jiū
凡	训	蒙，	须	讲	究。

xiáng	xùn	gǔ	míng	jù	dòu
详	训	诂，	明	句	读。

Original Text in Traditional Characters:

凡	訓	蒙，	須	講	究。
詳	訓	詁，	明	句	讀。

Notes:

训: to teach, to lecture

蒙: the ignorant, beginners, young children

究: to investigate

详: in details

训诂: to explain words in ancient texts

明: clearly, to make known

句读: punctuations, periods and commas, sentences and phrases

Modern Chinese:

对孩子进行启蒙教育的时候，必须采取严谨认真的态度，讲究教学方法。既要详细地解释文章里字词句的含义，也要讲明句子结构，便于理解。

三字經: 中華蒙學經典

Translation:

When teaching children in the beginning stage, one must be careful in research and teaching, and use effective instructional methods. The teacher must explain sentence structures and writing conventions so that the students may gain full comprehension.

Background information:

As an elementary primer, this chapter advises the proper instructional methodology. It argues for careful investigation and precise interpretation of the text. It also advises the teachers to help the students learn how to distinguish sentences and paragraphs of the text for comprehension, since traditional Chinese writing did not use punctuation marks. It was very difficult for the students to understand the text without knowing when and where a

孔子与弟子

sentence or a paragraph starts. Modern Chinese adopted punctuation marks from the western tradition later. The punctuation marks in modern Chinese are similar to those of English.

Chapter 28

Original Text in Simplified Characters:

wéi	xué	zhě	bì	yǒu	chū
为	学	者,	必	有	初。

xiǎo	xué	zhōng	zhì	sì	shū
小	学	终,	至	四	书。

Original Text in Traditional Characters:

為	學	者,	必	有	初。
小	學	終,	至	四	書。

Notes:

为: as, to become

小学: primary studies

终: to end

四书: Four Books

Modern Chinese:

读书求学的人一定都要从头开始，循序渐进。过去中国的读书人，先学称为"小学"的文字、训诂，再学被称为的"四书"的儒家典籍。（"四书"是指《论语》《孟子》《大学》《中庸》四种儒家典籍。）

Translation:

The curriculum sequence for a student was in a prescribed order in traditional education: one must start by learning the basics of character studies in literacy, then he can move on to study the Four Books of Confucius' classics.

Background information:

Since the Chinese language is not phonetic, but rather pictographic, children must learn the basic stroke orders and components of commonly used characters. Literacy education in traditional Chinese culture focuses on teaching children to memorize a large amount of characters before they read books. Not only will children learn hundreds and thousands of sight words, they also learn to trace, copy, and write these words. After the students learn the basics of Chinese characters and mastered literacy skills, they can move on to study other books.

The Four Books are: *The Analects of Confucius, Mencius, The Great Learning,* and *The Doctrine of the Mean.* They are four Confucian classics that introduce readers to the fundamental tenets of Confucianism.

Chapter 29

Original Text in Simplified Characters:

lún	yǔ	zhě	èr	shí	piān
论	语	者，	二	十	篇。

qún	dì	zǐ	jì	shàn	yán
群	弟	子，	记	善	言。

Original Text in Traditional Characters:

論	語	者，	二	十	篇。
群	弟	子，	記	善	言。

Notes:

论语: *The Analects of Confucius*

篇: chapters

群: a group of

弟子: disciples

记: to record   言: sayings, words

Modern Chinese:

《论语》这本书共有 20 篇，书中是孔子的弟子们记录孔子在讲学、论证、议事时饱含哲理的言论。

Translation:

There are 20 chapters in *The Analects of Confucius*, which was written by Confucius' disciples. The book recorded Confucius' wise sayings on various issues, including education, logic, government, virtue, and society.

三字經: 中華蒙學經典

Background information:

The Analects of Confucius is the most famous book of Confucian thought. Confucius (551–479 BCE) was born in the Spring and Autumn period into a poor family of noble origin. His Chinese name is Kong Qiu. People called him Kong Zi as a polite form, meaning Master Kong. The name "Confucius" was a Latin version of Kong Zi, coined by Matteo Ricci, one of the most well-known Jesuit missionaries to China in the Ming dynasty in the 16th century, who introduced him to Europe. Confucius' Golden Rule was found in the *Analects,* "Do not impose onto others what one does not wish on himself. *Ji suo bu yu, wu shi yu ren* 己所不欲，勿施于人." The book also contained descriptions of Confucius' personal life, including his behavior in court and with friends, as well as his pet peeves regarding sleeping and eating. For example, it was said that Confucius will not eat a meal without ginger. He also would not lie down on a mat that is not straight.

Confucius served as a government official in the State of Lu (current Shandong province in China) before he gave up the position and toured around different kingdoms in China, offering his advice to rulers. After his death, Confucius was deified, and Confucius Temples were erected in many places in China. Confucian thought was not only the dominant way of life in China, it also strongly influenced other Asian countries, including Japan, Korea, and Vietnam.

Chapter 30

Original Text in Simplified Characters:

mèng	zǐ	zhě	qī	piān	zhǐ
孟	子	者，	七	篇	止。

jiǎng	dào	dé	shuō	rén	yì
讲	道	德，	说	仁	义。

Original Text in Traditional Characters:

孟	子	者，	七	篇	止。
講	道	德，	說	仁	義。

Notes:

孟子: *Mencius*

止: to stop

道德: virtue, morality, ethics

仁义: benevolence and righteousness

Modern Chinese:

《孟子》这本书一共有七篇，书中讲的是孟子有关道德、仁义的学说和理念。

Translation:

There are seven chapters in the book *Mencius*. It talks about issues regarding virtue, love, and duty.

Background information:

Mencius (c. 372-289 BCE), by the Chinese name of Meng Ke or Meng Zi, Master Meng, was the foremost orthodox disciple of Confucian thought. Mencius lived during the Warring State period, and had Confucius' grandson Zisi as his teacher. Mencius further expounded on and perpetuated Confucianism. His philosophical work, *Mencius*, was considered as an important treaty on Confucianism. He was most well known for his argument that man's moral nature at birth is good, and it was due to external influences that man became either good or bad. However, man can realize his capacity of inborn good nature through studying and self-discipline. A famous historical anecdote was that Mengzi's mother relocated three times to choose the right neighborhood for him to have the right kind of influence in life (*meng mu san qian*, 孟母三迁). Like Confucius, Mencius also wandered around different regions in China in his time to offer his service to rulers.

Chapter 31

Original Text in Simplified Characters:

zuò	zhōng	yōng	zǐ	sī	bǐ
作	中	庸，	子	思	笔。
zhōng	bù	piān	yōng	bù	yì
中	不	偏，	庸	不	易。

Original Text in Traditional Characters:

作	中	庸，	子	思	筆。
中	不	偏，	庸	不	易。

Notes:

作: to compose, to write

中庸: *The Doctrine of the Mean*

笔: pen

偏: to incline to one side, to be partial, slanting,

庸: commonplace

易: to change

Modern Chinese:

《中庸》的作者是孔子的孙子子思。中是强调做人不偏激，庸是主张坚守真理不变易。（中庸主张的是儒家思想中做人要正直、诚实、尽责而不偏激的理念。）

Translation:

The book *The Doctrine of the Mean* was written by Zisi, Confucius' grandson. The central idea of this book advocates that a gentleman should be moderate and not be of extremes, and he should be steadfast in holding the principles without yielding.

Background information:

The Doctrine of the Mean was one of the four books selected by Zhu Xi, a neo-Confucian scholar of the Song dynasty, to be compiled in the *Four Books*, which became the Confucian canon that was used as standard curriculum for imperial examinations. The "doctrine of the mean" was translated by several sinologists and commentators into different terms. It was referred to as the "middle way" by Simon Leys; and the "constant mean" by James Legge. English author and poet Ezra Pound was also influenced by Confucianism and other classic Chinese literature. He referred to the "doctrine of the mean" as "the unwobbling pivot" in his book *Confucius: The Great Digest, The Unwobbling Pivot, The Analects*. The concept of the doctrine of the mean signifies an attitude and state of equilibrium and harmony. Anyone can achieve the middle way in any circumstance, as there is a right principle in all professions and in all situations. The idea of *zhong yong*, the doctrine of the mean, or the middle way, was used by Confucian scholars as a chief principle in personal conduct and the cultivation of virtues in the tumultuous society.

Chapter 32

Original Text in Simplified Characters:

zuò	dà	xué	nǎi	zēng	zǐ
作	大	学，	乃	曾	子。

zì	xiū	qí	zhì	píng	zhì
自	修	齐，	至	平	治。

Original Text in Traditional Characters:

作	大	學，	乃	曾	子。
自	修	齊，	至	平	治。

Notes:

大学: *The Great Learning*

乃: to be

自: from

修: to prune, to discipline oneself

齐: to bring order

至: to

平: to bring peace to the world

治: to govern, to manage

Modern Chinese:

《大学》这本书是孔子的学生曾子所写。这本书论述了一个人应先从提高自身修养做起，把家庭管理好，然后才可以治理国家，最后实现天下太平。这个道理就是"修身、齐家、治国、平天下。"

Translation:

The Great Learning was written by one of Confucius' disciples Zengzi. This book explains how people should start from cultivating themselves and managing their families well, then move on to govern their country wisely, and eventually bring peace to the world.

Background information:

The Great Learning is also one of the *Four Books* complied by Zhu Xi in the Song dynasty to convey major Confucian ideas and was used as part of the curriculum for imperial examinations from the 12th to 19th centuries. *The Great Learning* was most well known for its Eight Categories of conduct that outline the progression of how one can learn and cultivate oneself to reach the ultimate goal of bringing world peace. The Eight Categories are to investigate all areas of life, therefore, one is to be acquiring knowledge, have a sincere will, and have a righteous heart; to be cultivating oneself, bringing order to family, governing the country, then bringing peace to the

world (*ge wu, zhi zhi, cheng yi, zheng xin, xiu shen, qi jia, zhi guo, ping tian xia* 格物、致知、诚意、正心、修身、齐家、治国、平天下). Among these Eight Categories, the last four were even more well-known: self-cultivation, managing one's family, governing the country, and bringing world peace.

三字經: 中華蒙學經典

Chapter 33

Original Text in Simplified Characters:

xiào	jīng	tōng	sì	shū	shóu
孝	经	通，	四	书	熟。

rú	liù	jīng	shǐ	kě	dú
如	六	经，	始	可	读。

Original Text in Traditional Characters:

孝	經	通，	四	書	熟。
如	六	經，	始	可	讀。

Notes:

孝经: *The Book of Filial Piety*

通: to understand

熟: to be familiar with, to be skilled in

如: such as

始: to begin

Modern Chinese:

读书的顺序是这样的：应该先读儒家论述孝道的《孝经》，
明白孝敬父母的道理，再熟读"四书"，明白做人的道理，
然后才可以开始研读"六经"。

Translation:

The curriculum sequence for learning should be like this: the
students must first read *The Book of Filial Piety*, understanding

the proper ways of respecting their parents; then proceed to read *The Four Books*, understanding how to live a righteous life; and finally, they could continue to read the Six Classics.

Background information:

The Book of Filial Piety was written by Confucius. It enumerates reasons and proper ways of respecting one's parents. *The Four Books* are: *The Analects, Mencius, The Doctrine of the Mean,* and *The Great Learning.* The four books were compiled by the neo-Confucian scholar Zhu Xi in the Song dynasty as the official Confucian canon for students to study for the imperial examinations.

孔子为曾参等讲述孝道

The Confucian classics were initially introduced to the West in Latin by Matteo Ricci, who served as a Jesuit Missionary in China in the 16th century. Ricci learned Chinese and became a Confucian scholar, whose knowledge of Classic Chinese was admired by the Chinese scholars at his time. James Legge, a Scottish missionary to China in the 19th century, also introduced much of the Chinese works, including Confucian classics to the West by translating them into English.

Chapter 34

Original Text in Simplified Characters:

shī	shū	yì	lǐ	chūn	qiū
诗	书	易，	礼	春	秋。

hào	liù	jīng	dāng	jiǎng	qiú
号	六	经，	当	讲	求。

Original Text in Traditional Characters:

詩	書	易，	禮	春	秋。
號	六	經，	當	講	求。

Notes:

诗: *Book of Poetry*

书: *Book of History*

易: *Book of Changes*

礼: *Rites of Zhou* and *Book of Rites*

春秋: *Spring and Autumn Annals*

当: ought to

讲求: to study and understand

Modern Chinese:

《诗经》、《尚书》、《易经》、《周礼》、《仪礼》和《春秋》
合称为六经。学子们应该认真学习和研究。

Translation:

The Book of Poetry, Book of History, Book of Changes, Rites of Zhou, Book of Rites, and *The Spring and Autumn Annals* are referred to as the Six Classics. Students should study and examine these six books carefully.

Background information:

The Book of Poetry, or *Shi Jing,* is also referred to as *The Book of Odes,* or *The Book of Songs,* which was a collection of various genres of poems that were considered the earliest creation of Chinese literature. While it is debatable, some believe Confucius was the complier of the book. *The Book of Poetry* was conjured with vivid metaphors and imagery, serving as the foundation for Chinese literature in later generations. It was written to be sung aloud. Confucius commented that the content of *The Book of Poetry* was pure, *Yi yi yan yi bi zhi, si wu xie* 以一言以蔽之，思无邪. After one reads it, they should learn to think no evil.

The Book of History, or *Shang Shu,* and *The Spring and Autumn Annals,* or *Chun Qiu,* were also books edited or written by Confucius. *The Book of History* recorded early Chinese oral history while *The Spring and Autumn Annals* documented the history of the Lu state, where Confucius was from, during the Spring and Autumn periods.

The Rites of Zhou, or *Zhou Li,* and *The Book of Rites,* or *Yi Li,* were books regarding proper protocols in various state ceremonies and appropriate social as well as personal etiquettes practiced in ancient China.

The Book of Changes, or *Yi Jing,* was a book of divination, containing many coded languages and symbols.

These six books are also called the Six Classics, which later were referred to as the Five Classics (*The Rites of Zhou* was dismissed in the Ming dynasty). These, along with the Four Books, were the standard curriculum for traditional Chinese education.

Chapter 35

Original Text in Simplified Characters:

yǒu	lián	shān	yǒu	guī	cáng
有	连	山，	有	归	藏。

yǒu	zhōu	yì	sān	yì	xiáng
有	周	易，	三	易	详。

Original Text in Traditional Characters:

有	連	山，	有	歸	藏。
有	周	易，	三	易	詳。

Notes:

连山: *Book of Lian Shan*

归藏: *Book of Gui Cang*

周易: *Book of Changes*

详: detail

Modern Chinese:

《易经》一书有三个版本：《连山》、《归藏》和《周易》。
(《连山》相传为伏羲所作；《归藏》相传是黄帝所作；
《周易》相传是文王周公、孔子所作。)

Translation:

The Book of Changes has three versions: *Lian Shan*, *Gui Cang*, and *Zhou Yi*.

Background information:

The Book of Changes is also called *I Ching*. The Chinese word for I, *yi*, means "easy or change." *The Book of Changes* is about how to understand the changes in every situation in life and also to be flexible according to the changes. The book contains 64 symbols, also called the hexagram, which served as guiding themes for all situations and were used in divination. The book has a close relationship with the Taoism concept about the balance of yin and yang. Although a concise book, as its name implies that the mystery of the universe is indeed very simple, it is most abstruse to those who are not familiar with the meaning of the symbols. Great minds in history, including Confucius, have studied it and commented on it. It is the oldest book among the Six Classics, and the oldest philosophical text of all Chinese books.

The Book of Lian Shan is said to be the first edition of *The Book of Changes*. Its author was Fu Xi, a figure in ancient Chinese mythology who taught human beings fishing. The legend said that he was inspired by a sign he saw on the back of a tortoise, and invented *bagua*, the trigram, which served as foundation for the hexagrams in the later versions of *The Book of Changes*.

The Book of Gui Cang is the second edition of *The Book of Changes*. Its author was the Yellow Emperor, who was a legendary king in Chinese oral history.

The first two books, *Lian Shan* and *Gui Cang*, were lost to history. The current version of *The Book of Changes* was written by the Duke of Zhou in the Zhou dynasty. Confucius also added his commentary to the book. Based on this version, modern scholars continue to study *The Book of Changes*.

Chapter 36

Original Text in Simplified Characters:

yǒu	diǎn	mó	yǒu	xùn	gào
有	典	谟，	有	训	诰。

yǒu	shì	mìng	shū	zhī	ào
有	誓	命，	书	之	奥。

Original Text in Traditional Characters:

有	典	謨，	有	訓	誥。
有	誓	命，	書	之	奥。

Notes:

典: standards

谟: consuls

训: advice

诰: imperial commands

誓: oath, pledges

命: orders   奥: mystery

Modern Chinese:

《尚书》是很深奥的典籍，其中有典、谟、训、诰、誓、命各种内容。(《尚书》也叫《书经》。这本书记录了上古到西周的历史文献，内容非常深奥。它的篇名有典、谟、训、诰、誓、命。"典"写的是帝王应遵守的常道；"谟"是大臣献谋的计策；"训"是大臣对君王的进谏；"诰"是君主发出的命令；"誓"是君主征战前的誓言；"命"是帝王下达的命令。)

Translation:

The Book of History is a very erudite classical text, which contains topics on ancient governmental principles, advice, instructions, announcements, mandates, and the oaths of the King and his ministers.

Background information:

The Book of History is also called *The Book of Documents*. It attributes the authorship to Confucius, who complied ancient Chinese history from the legendary King Yao to the last king of the Western Zhou dynasty. Different chapters of the book recorded various historical occasions regarding the principles of government that kings should follow, the counsels of ministers to the kings, kings' instructions, announcements, and mandates to his ministers and subjects, as well as the oaths taken before battles.

The Book of History was written in classical Chinese, its content dealt with subjects of a complex historical nature, and it is not a commonly studied book among modern Chinese readers.

Chapter 37

Original Text in Simplified Characters:

wǒ	zhōu	gōng	zuò	zhōu	lǐ
我	周	公，	作	周	礼。

zhù	liù	guān	cún	zhì	tǐ
著	六	官，	存	治	体。

三字經: 中華蒙學經典

Original Text in Traditional Characters:

我	周	公,	作	周	禮。
著	六	官,	存	治	體。

Notes:

周公: Duke of the Zhou dynasty

周礼: *The Rites of Zhou*

官: government officials, ministries

存: to preserve

治: ruling, governing

体: body, systems

Modern Chinese:

《周礼》相传为周公所作，其中列举六种官府内各种官员的职务和责任。（周文王的儿子周公，也叫姬旦，写了《周礼》一书，记载了当时设立的六个政府机构。 六官即六卿，分别为天官、地官、春官、吏官、秋官、冬官，掌管国家的各项行政，为当时及以后的政治体系奠定了基础。）

Translation:

The Duke of Zhou wrote *The Rites of Zhou*. The book recorded the establishment of six governmental offices, listing their functions and responsibilities. They kept the government running well and served as foundations for future political institutions.

Background information:

The six government offices are six government ministries.

Their names were Office of Heaven, Office of Earth, and Offices of Spring, Summer, Autumn, and Winter, respectively. The function of the Office of Heaven was equivalent to today's State Department, managing state affairs in general; the Office of Earth was responsible for education, similar to today's Department of Education; the Office of Spring focused on social and religious ceremonies and institutions; the Office of Summer was comparable to the Department of Defense; the Office of Autumn was like the Justice Department; the Office of Winter resembled the U.S. Department of the Interior, which was responsible for agricultural and other interior matters.

Chapter 38

Original Text in Simplified Characters:

dà	xiǎo	dài	zhù	lǐ	jì
大	小	戴,	注	礼	记。

shù	shèng	yán	lǐ	yuè	bèi
述	圣	言,	礼	乐	备。

Original Text in Traditional Characters:

大	小	戴,	注	禮	記。
述	聖	言,	禮	樂	備。

Notes:

戴: Dai, a last name

注: to make comments, to annotate

礼记: *The Book of Rites*

三字經: 中華蒙學經典

述: to narrate, to relate

圣: sages

言: words, sayings

备: complete

Modern Chinese:

汉朝时有两位儒学学者，戴德，也称大戴，戴圣，也称小戴。他们分别编辑注释了《礼经》一书，阐述了圣人先贤言论的意义，提供了圣贤的贵族参加各种政治和社会活动应当具备的礼仪和乐舞规范。

Translation:

There were two Han dynasty Confucius scholars by the names of Dai De, also called Big Dai, and Dai Sheng, referred to as Little Dai. They edited *The Book of Rites,* explaining the meaning of sages' words, outlining the standard for proper music and dances, as well as ceremonial protocols required at various political and social occasions.

Background information:

In 213 BCE during the Qin dynasty, Emperor Qin Shihuang ordered philosophical books, including Confucian classics, to be burnt to get rid of their influence in his kingdom, only books regarding agriculture, medicine, and divination were spared. He also had many scholars who were suspected of different political and philosophical views buried alive (*fen shu keng ru,* 焚书坑儒). Confucianism was banned in the Qin dynasty, and legalism was the official philosophy. However, beginning with the following Han dynasty, Confucianism was revived, and Confucian books were recompiled. Therefore, Dai De and Dai Sheng were the scholars who edited *The Book of Rites*, one of the Confucian classics, for their contemporaries and later generations to study. Since then, Confucian thought has been the state-sanctioned philosophy in imperial China, and has remained as the dominant philosophy and way of life in Chinese culture.

Chapter 39

Original Text in Simplified Characters:

yuē	guó	fēng	yuē	yǎ	sòng
曰	国	风,	曰	雅	颂。
hào	sì	shī	dāng	fěng	yǒng
号	四	诗,	当	讽	咏。

Original Text in Traditional Characters:

曰	國	風,	曰	雅	頌。
號	四	詩,	當	諷	咏。

Notes:

曰: to speak of, to say

国风: Lessons of the States, a section in *The Book of Poetry*

雅: Odes of the Kingdom, a section in *The Book of Poetry*

颂: Odes for Temples and Altars, a section in *The Book of Poetry*

讽咏: to chant, to read aloud with intonation

Modern Chinese:

《诗经》一书有四部分，分别是国风，大雅，小雅和颂。
因此也称"四诗"，学习诗经时应当反复诵读吟唱。

　　　　　　　三字經: 中華蒙學經典

Translation:

The Book of Poetry has four sections: the Lessons of the States, Major Odes of the Kingdom, Lesser Odes of the Kingdom, and Odes for Temples and Altars. Therefore it is also referred as "Four Poetry." The book should be chanted and sung aloud for recitation and memorization.

Background information:

As the earliest Chinese literature, *The Book of Poetry* contains the four sections that are about four different subjects. The Lessons of the States contains folk songs collected from various states of China, which reflected the customs and affairs of those states; Major and Minor Odes of the Kingdom are songs sung at formal and general gatherings of the aristocrats; the Odes for the Temples and Altars are songs sung at religious ceremonies.

The lyrics in *The Book of Poetry* are very beautiful. They were cited by poets and literary scholars in their works up to the present time. Memorization of *The Book of Poetry* and other classics was expected in traditional Chinese literary culture. A popular mnemonic device to help with memorization was to chant and sing the content aloud. Chinese students use this method to remember, not only literature, but also the multiplication table and other information required.

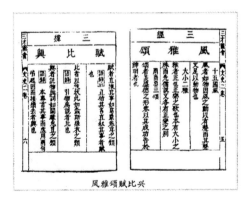

風雅頌賦比興

Chapter 40

Original Text in Simplified Characters:

shī	jì	wáng	chūn	qiū	zuò
诗	既	亡，	春	秋	作。
yù	bāo	biǎn	bié	shàn	è
寓	褒	贬，	别	善	恶。

Original Text in Traditional Characters:

詩	既	亡，	春	秋	作。
寓	褒	貶，	別	善	惡。

Notes:

既: already

亡: dead, discontinued

寓: to imply

褒: praise

貶: blame, condemnation

別: to distinguish, to differentiate

善惡: good and evil

Modern Chinese:

《诗经》的时代结束后，孔子整理鲁国史书《春秋》，记录了鲁国君王二百四十二年的历史，书中评论各个君王的作为，有加以表扬的，也有加以批评的，籍此帮助世人和后人区分和甄别政事的善恶。

Translation:

After the period of *The Book of Poetry*, Confucius compiled *The Spring and Autumn Annals*, a history book for the region of Lu. This book chronicled about 240 years of the history of Lu, in which he evaluated every ruler's performance, praising some while condemning others, so that people may learn to distinguish good from bad government.

Background information:

The words "Spring and Autumn, or Chun Qiu" mean time and history in general, as the Spring and Autumn are passages of seasons from year to year. It also implies the supreme power of rulers, who have the authority to kill and let live, just as spring brings life and autumn brings death to nature.

In the book *Spring and Autumn Annals*, Confucius recorded the history between 722 BCE and 481 BCE in the region of Lu from a distinct perspective, as he implied praise and condemnation to certain kings. Even though he intended to criticize a king, he could not do so bluntly, but rather through metaphors and allegories. The communication style in Chinese culture is indirect, rather than direct. Ministers and subjects often use metaphors and satires to admonish kings, rulers, and others in higher positions.

Chapter 41

Original Text in Simplified Characters:

sān	zhuàn	zhě	yǒu	gōng	yáng
三	传	者,	有	公	羊。

yǒu	zuǒ	shì	yǒu	gǔ	liáng
有	左	氏,	有	谷	梁。

Original Text in Traditional Characters:

三　傳　者，　有　公　羊。
有　左　氏，　有　谷　梁。

Notes:

传: commentary

公羊: Gongyang, a last name

左: Zuo, a last name

氏: family-name, surname

谷梁: Guliang, a last name

Modern Chinese:

对《春秋》一书加以注释的书主要有三种，分别是公羊高写的《公羊传》，左丘明写的《左传》和谷梁赤写的《谷梁传》。（传是解释"经"的书。经是古代圣人，如孔子、孟子等写的书。前面所说的包括四书六经。注释《春秋》的"三传"中，《左传》的注释最有名，也称《左氏春秋》。）

Translation:

There are three commentaries on *The Spring and Autumn Annals*. There were *Gongyang Zhuan*, also called *The Commentary of Gongyang*, written by Gongyang Gao; *Zuo Zhuan, The Commentary of Zuo* by Zuo Qiuming; and *Gulian Zhuan, The Commentary of Gulian* by Guliang Chi.

Background information:

In the Chinese language, the word *jing* refers to a classic written by the sages of ancient times, such as the Four Books and Six Classics mentioned in earlier chapters. The word *zhuan* refers to commentaries written to explain the classics. The

三字經：中華蒙學經典

character for *jing* 经 is made up of a thread radical and another component meaning "road or course"; together it means "constant, through, endure," and, therefore, implying a "canon or classic;" the Chinese word for *zhuan* 传 is made up of a person radical and another component meaning "to specialize." The word *zhuan* means "biography," or "a novel written in historical style," or "commentaries on the classics."

Among the three classics on *The Spring and Autumn Annals*, *The Commentary of Zuo* is most distinguished. It is also called *Zuo Shi Chun Qiu, The Chronicle of Zuo*. It is an excellent record of the history of Spring and Autumn period in its own right.

Chapter 42

Original Text in Simplified Characters:

jīng	jì	míng	fāng	dú	zǐ
经	既	明,	方	读	子。
cuō	qí	yào	jì	qí	shì
撮	其	要,	记	其	事。

Original Text in Traditional Characters:

經	既	明,	方	讀	子。
撮	其	要,	記	其	事。

Notes:

明: to understand

子: philosophers

撮: to father, to extract

要: essentials, important part

Modern Chinese:

经书读懂之后，才可以读诸子百家，因为诸子百家的书
籍繁多，读这些书时，应该取其精华，挑选其中重要的
部分阅览，并刻意记住书中有关的事例。

Translation:

After comprehending the Six Classics, a student can begin to
read philosophical books. Because there are numerous books
on various schools of thought, it is better to peruse the core
segment selectively, and memorize related information.

Background information:

Hundreds of Schools of Thought was a period before the
Qin dynasty when various philosophical schools of thought
flourished in China. During the Spring and Autumn and Warring States period (770-221 BCE), China was divided into different states where feudal lords competed with each other at-
tempting to control and unite the country. Scholars, philosophers, diplomats, and military strategists wandered from state
to state trying to sell their ideas and consul rulers and lords.
This was a golden age for uninhibited philosophical and intellectual development in China. Some of the prominent schools
of thought were Confucianism, Taoism, Legalism, Mohism,
School of Yin-yang and Five Elements, School of Vertical
and Horizontal Alliance, School of Agriculture, School of
Military, School of Logicians, Miscellaneous School, and
School of Minor-talks. After Emperor Qin Shihuang united
China in 221 BCE, he adopted Legalism as the state philoso-
phy and abolished other schools of thought through the infamous historical event of Burning Books and Burying
Scholars period in 231 BCE. Many of the philosophical books

were destroyed during that time. After the Han dynasty, Confucianism was adopted as a state philosophy by Chinese emperors. Taoism was also widely studied by scholars since then.

Chapter 43

Original Text in Simplified Characters:

wǔ	zǐ	zhě	yǒu	xún	yáng
五	子	者，	有	荀	杨。

wén	zhōng	zǐ	jí	lǎo	zhuāng
文	中	子，	及	老	庄。

Original Text in Traditional Characters:

五	子	者，	有	荀	楊。
文	中	子，	及	老	莊。

Notes:

老庄: Laozi and Zhuangzi, two Taoist philosophers

Modern Chinese:

诸子百家中最有名的五子为：荀子、杨子、文中子、老子和庄子。（他们的著作分别为周朝荀子的《荀子》；汉朝杨雄杨子的《法言》和《太玄经》；隋朝的王道文中子的《中说》和《元经》；周朝李耳老子的《道德经》，也叫《老子》；周朝庄周庄子的《南华经》。）

Translation:

Among the Hundred Schools of Thought, the five most prominent philosophers were Xun Zi, Yang Zi, Wenzhong Zi, Lao Zi, and Zhuang Zi.

Background information:

Xun Zi (312-230 BCE) was a philosopher during the Eastern

Zhou dynasty, whose work is known as *Xu Zi*. Although a Confucian philosopher, unlike Mencius who argued for man's innate good nature, Xun Zi suggested that man's nature was prone to evil and it had to be curbed to be good. One of his disciples was Li Si, who became the prime minister of the Qin dynasty. Li Si practiced Legalism and brought harsh rule to the people of Qin.

Yang Zi was Yang Xiong, a philosopher and linguist in the Han dynasty. He was a very talented individual who devoted himself to the study of Confucianism and Taoism. He wrote two philosophical books, *Fa Yan*, modeling after *The Analects of Confucius*, and *The Book of Tai Xuan*, modeling after Lao Zi's *Dao De Jing*.

Wengzhong Zi, also known as Wang Dao, was a philosopher in the Sui dynasty, who wrote the books *Zhong Shuo* and *Yuan Jing*.

Lao Zi is called Li Er, founder of Taoism who was a philosopher in the Zhou dynasty. Lao Zi wrote the book *Dao De Jing (Tao Te Ching)*, also referred as *Lao Zi*. Zhuang Zi was Lao Zi's important disciple, who wrote *Nan Hua Jing*.

Among the five philosophers, Lao Zi and Zhuang Zi were most recognized and commonly studied.

Chapter 44

Original Text in Simplified Characters:

jīng	zǐ	tōng	dú	zhū	shǐ
经	子	通，	读	诸	史。

kǎo	shì	xì	zhī	zhōng	shǐ
考	世	系，	知	终	始。

Original Text in Traditional Characters:

經	子	通，	讀	諸	史。
考	世	系，	知	終	始。

Notes:

通: to go through, to understand

諸: various, all

史: history books

考: to examine

世: generation

系: relations, systems

Modern Chinese:

经书和子书都读通了，就可以阅读各种史书。这样可以考证历代帝王承传的世代系统，了解历史事件的始末。

Translation:

After mastering the classics and major works in philosophy, students can read various history books. This will help them examine the genealogical connections of emperors in various

三字經: 中華蒙學經典

dynasties, and understand the beginning and ending of major historical events.

Background information:

The emperor of China was called "Son of Heaven," suggesting that he represents supreme authority from heaven to rule the country. Not only were the emperors considered head of China, but also they assumed leadership in the world, with China being at its center. Even though the emperors were not deified, they were considered to be above all in the kingdom. Their names were never to be addressed directly by anyone, including their own mother. Emperors were to be diligent and should serve their people well. They also had to apply themselves to study constantly. Ministers had the right and responsibility to consul and admonish the emperor. Even though emperors were general hereditary to allow the line of succession to continue within their family, there were incidents in history when emperors were too cruel or licentious to be considered fit by the people. Rebellions took place and new dynasties were founded. One of the most prominent dynasties in China, the Ming dynasty, was found by Zhu Yuanzhang, who was a peasant without noble origin. Mongolians and Manchurians took over China in the Yuan and Qing dynasties, and established non-Han Chinese emperors during those periods. However, they eventually become sinicized.

Part Three

(Chpaters 45-71)

Chinese History

Chapter 45

Original Text in Simplified Characters:

zì	xī	nóng	zhì	huáng	dì
自	羲	农，	至	黄	帝。

hào	sān	huáng	jū	shàng	shì
号	三	皇，	居	上	世。

Original Text in Traditional Characters:

自	羲	農，	至	黃	帝。
號	三	皇，	居	上	世。

Notes:

羲: Fu Xi, Emperor Fu Xi

农: Sheng Nong, Emperor Sheng Nong

黄帝: The Yellow Emperor

号: to be called, to be known as

皇: sovereigns

居: to live

Modern Chinese:

从伏羲，神农到黄帝，他们被称为"三皇"，都是上古时期的君主。

Translation:

Fu Xi, Sheng Nong, and the Yellow Emperor are called "The Three Sovereigns." They were sovereigns of antiquity.

Background information:

Fu Xi (Cir. 2800 BCE) was a mythological creature in Chinese  culture. He was depicted as a man with a snake body in ancient Chinese art. The legend says he married his sister, Nuwa, a woman with a snake body, and human beings came from them. Fu Xi invented fishing and *bagua*, the trigrams with symbolic meanings.

Sheng Nong (Cir. 2700 BCE) was also a mythological creature in Chinese culture, who invented agriculture. He was referred to as Yan Di, and, together with the Yellow Emperor, they were considered as the ancestors of Han Chinese people.

The Yellow Emperor was a mythological creature as well, although his birth place and tomb were identified to exist in China. The Yellow Emperor invented traditional Chinese medicine, while his wife invented sericulture—the production of silk from silk worms. Every year, many Chinese in China and overseas go to visit the tombs of the Yellow Emperor to pay homage.

Chapter 46

Original Text in Simplified Characters:

táng	yǒu	yú	hào	èr	dì
唐	有	虞，	号	二	帝。

xiāng	yī	xùn	chēng	shèng	shì
相	揖	逊，	称	盛	世。

三字經: 中華蒙學經典

Original Text in Traditional Characters:

唐	有	虞，	號	二	帝。
相	揖	遜，	稱	盛	世。

Notes:

有虞: Yu Shun, King Shun

揖: to bow

遜: to abdicate

盛: prosperous, grand

世: age, era

Modern Chinese:

上古时唐尧和虞舜号称"二帝"，他们两个人彼此尊重敬佩，退位后都把帝位禅让给贤人，而没有传给自己的儿子。他们统治的时代被称为太平盛世。（唐尧把帝位传给舜，就是舜帝。虞舜把帝位禅让给了大禹。）

Translation:

In antiquity, Tang Yao and Yu Shun were called two kings. They respected each other, and both gave the crown to virtuous individuals rather than their sons when they abdicated their thrones. The era of their reigns was called "the age of prosperity."

Background information:

Tang Yao and Yu Shun, also known as You Yu or Da Shun, were legendary kings and heroes in Chinese oral history. Both leaders were known for their great virtues and altruism. Tao Yao lived a very modest life, and had much compassion for his subjects. His administration was open to the public. It was said that he established "Commentary Columns" along the roadside, where any commoner could approach the Commentary Columns, petitioning his case to the officers stationed by the columns, and have his case reported to the king. The tradition of Commentary Columns was also used in later dynasties as a venue for public voice. However, it gradually lost its original function, and its name was also changed from the original *bang mu* (commentary wood 谤木) to *hua biao* (Chinese Exterior 华表). Different forms of *hua biao* served road signs and time pieces in history. They were mainly used as architectural decoration in front of palaces and tombs. With ornate dragon designs and elaborate cloud patterns, they serve as icons of Chinese culture today.

Shun was also known for his virtue. He was especially known for his filial piety to his parents. Legend says that Shun had a cruel stepmother, but he never held grudges against her and was always forgiving and kind to her and his father.

Instead of having their sons inherit the throne, Tang Yao gave the crown to Shun, and Shun later gave the crown to Da Yu. However, from Da Yu on, all Chinese emperors had their sons or relatives inherit the throne.

Chapter 47

Original Text in Simplified Characters:

xià	yǒu	yǔ	shāng	yǒu	tāng
夏	有	禹,	商	有	汤。

zhōu	wén	wǔ	chēng	sān	wáng
周	文	武,	称	三	王。

三字經: 中華蒙學經典

Original Text in Traditional Characters:

夏	有	禹,	商	有	湯。
周	文	武,	稱	三	王。

Notes:

夏: the Xia dynasty

商: the Shang dynasty

周: the Zhou dynasty

文: King Wen of the Zhou dynasty

武: King Zhou of the Zhou dynasty

王: King

Modern Chinese:

夏朝的开国皇帝叫禹，就是大禹治水的禹。商朝的开国皇帝叫成汤，历史上称他为商汤。周朝的开国皇帝为周武王，他封他的父亲为周文王，（因为周朝建立时周文王已经过世，所以周文王和周武王被并称为周文武。）禹、汤、文武被称为"三王"。

Translation:

The founding emperor of the Xia dynasty was called Yu, who was known for his work in flood management. The founding emperor for the Shang dynasty was called Cheng Tang, who was also referred to as Shang Tang. King Wu of Zhou and his father King Wen of Zhou, titled posthumously, established the Zhou dynasty. Yu, Cheng Tang, and Kings Wu and Wen of Zhou were called the Three Kings.

Background information:

Dynasties are historical periods in China during which different families ruled China. The Xia dynasty is the first dynasty in China when the founder/emperor Da Yu or Yu the Great gave the throne to his son Qi. Little is known about Xia as there are not many archeological findings about the era. Some historians consider this period as mythology. There are many legends about Yu the Great. As in many cultures, China also has a flood tale. Yu was the hero who successfully engineered flood control in ancient China. He was known for his altruistic act when he had three occasions to stop by his house during the busy work of his flood control project; he chose not to enter because he vowed to finish his work first.

On the other hand, a plethora of artifacts has been uncovered about the history and culture of the Shang dynasty. The oracle bones, tortoise shells and cow blades with writings on them, indicated the earliest findings of Chinese characters during this period. The Shang dynasty was known about from its highly advanced civilization evidenced in its bronze technology, written language, religious and political rituals, social organizations, astronomy, and medicine.

The Zhou dynasty also had a rich written history, during which bronze technology was further developed, philosophy flourished, and other political and social institutions became more established.

Chapter 48

Original Text in Simplified Characters:

xià	chuán	zǐ	jiā	tiān	xià
夏	传	子，	家	天	下。

三字經: 中華蒙學經典

sì	bǎi	zǎi	qiān	xià	shè
四	百	载，	迁	夏	社。

Original Text in Traditional Characters:

夏	傳	子，	家	天	下。
四	百	載，	遷	夏	社。

Notes:

天下: land under heaven, the world

载: years

社: society

Modern Chinese:

从夏朝开始大禹将帝位直接传给儿子，改变了以前帝王
禅位于贤人的政治体系，因此夏朝以后称为"家天下"，
（就是天下是"一家"的天下。）夏朝持续了四百年后就灭
亡了。

Translation:

In the Xia dynasty, Yu the Great gave the throne to his son, and established familial dynastic cycles; hence he initiated a new hereditary political system, contrasting to previous times where the power was passed to individuals of virtue and merit. The Xia dynasty lasted for four hundred years.

Background information:

Before the Xia dynasty, the political system in China was called *guan tian xia* 官天下, meaning the official rule under heaven; the Three Sovereigns and Five Kings ruled the country without selfish motives, and all abdicated the throne to those that best served the country's interests. Since the Xia dynasty, the political system changed to *jia tian xia* 家天下, family rule under heaven, starting the hereditary system for emperor successions. The Chinese emperor addressed his kingdom as *tian xia*, which literally means "under heaven," implying his reign was not only over the Chinese empire, but also everywhere on earth.

Chapter 49

Original Text in Simplified Characters:

tāng	fá	xià	guó	hào	shāng
汤	伐	夏，	国	号	商。

liù	bǎi	zǎi	zhì	zhòu	wáng
六	百	载，	至	纣	亡。

Original Text in Traditional Characters:

湯	伐	夏，	國	號	商。
六	百	載，	至	紂	亡。

Notes:

汤: King Cheng Tang

伐: to cut down, to strike

国号: to name the dynasty as

纣: King Zhou of Shang

Modern Chinese:

夏朝的最后一个皇帝为夏桀，是历史上罕见的暴君。成

汤带领民众讨伐夏桀，建立了新的国家成为商朝。商朝
持续了六百年，到纣王时灭亡。

Translation:

The last emperor of the Xia dynasty was King Jie, who was a
licentious tyrant. Cheng Tang led the people in rebellion,
abolished Jie of Xia and established a new dynasty named
Shang. Shang lasted for six hundred years, and ended with the
reign of King Zhou.

Background information:

King Jie of Xia was a tyrant. During his reign, abnormal
weather caused the traditional agricultural China society many
disasters. Instead of governing the country with diligence, Jie
indulged himself in women and wine, including building a
wine lake for boating and pleasure.

Cheng Tang was a wise tribal leader, who defeated King
Jie, and sent him into exile. King Tang established the Shang
dynasty.

Chapter 50

Original Text in Simplified Characters:

zhōu	wǔ	wáng	shǐ	zhū	zhòu
周	武	王，	始	诛	纣。
bā	bǎi	zǎi	zuì	cháng	jiǔ
八	百	载，	最	长	久。

Original Text in Traditional Characters:

周　武　王，　始　誅　紂。
八　百　載，　最　長　久。

Notes:

誅: to kill, to punish, to put to death

最: most

長久: long duration

Modern Chinese:

商纣王是历史上一个有名的暴君，昏庸无道。周武王率领诸侯讨伐纣王，建立了周朝。周朝一共持续了八百多年，是中国历史上最长久的朝代。

Translation:

King Zhou of Shang was an infamous tyrant with a reputation for extraordinary cruelty and wickedness in Chinese history. King Wu led the dukes and noblemen in a crusade against King Zhou, and established the new Zhou dynasty, which was the longest dynasty in Chinese history, lasting for eight hundred years.

Background information:

King Zhou of Shang was one of the most notorious tyrants in Chinese history. In addition to a wine lake, King Zhou also created a meat forest where roasted meat hung from tree branches, and where King Zhou indulged in pleasure and sensuality with his concubines and officials. King Zhou also devised a torturing method called "cannon burning punishment, *pao luo zhi xing* 炮烙之刑," whereas both prisoners and righteous ministers who challenged him were forced to walk on rows of slowly-heated-bronze cylinders as punishment. While the prisoners struggled to jump from cylinders to cylinders, and inevitably fell to the burning charcoals below in the end, King Zhou and his consort derived much pleasure in seeing the agony of the poor souls.

King Wu of Shang succeeded his father King Wen's endeavor and defeated King Zhou.

A classic Chinese novel, *Fengshen Yanyi* 封神演义 *(Creation of Gods)*, was based on the decline of the Shang dynasty and the rise of the Zhou dynasty.

Ancient Warfare

Chapter 51

Original Text in Simplified Characters:

zhōu	zhé	dōng	wáng	gāng	zhuì
周	辙	东，	王	纲	坠。

chěng	gān	gē	shàng	yóu	shuì
逞	干	戈，	尚	游	说。

Original Text in Traditional Characters:

周	辙	東，	王	綱	墜。
逞	干	戈，	尚	游	説。

Notes:

辙: the track of wheels, here implying to move

王纲: the guiding principle of kingship, governing systems

墜: degenerate

逞: to show off

干戈: weapons

尚: to esteem, to value

游说: persuasion, going about selling ideas

Modern Chinese:

周朝东迁洛阳之后，王室衰弱，朝政和法纪混乱。各诸侯国称王，彼此逞强打仗；文士们到处游说，向掌权者推荐自己的策略和主张。（周朝分为西周和东周。西周的都城在西部的镐京，即现在的西安附近；东周时迁都到东部的洛阳。）

Translation:

When the Zhou dynasty relocated its capital eastward to Luoyang, court administration and legal systems deteriorated. Regional warlords competed for control of the country with military power. Itinerant scholars wandered from state to state, petitioning rulers and selling their ideas and strategies.

Background information:

The Zhou dynasty was divided into Western Zhou, with its capital in Haojing, near today's Xi'an, and Eastern Zhou, with its capital in Luoyang. Barbarian attacks from the north and internal rebellions forced the Zhou dynasty to move its capital eastward to Luoyang, which is in interior China.

周平王东迁

Chapter 52

Original Text in Simplified Characters:

shǐ	chūn	qiū	zhōng	zhàn	guó
始	春	秋,	终	战	国。

wǔ	bà	qiáng	qī	xióng	chū
五	霸	强,	七	雄	出。

Original Text in Traditional Characters:

始	春	秋,	終	戰	國。
五	霸	強,	七	雄	出。

Notes:

春秋: the Spring and Autumn period

战国: the Warring States period

霸: chief of feudal princes

强: strong

雄: powerful states

Modern Chinese:

东周的前期称为春秋，后期称为战国。春秋是有五个强大的诸侯，称为春秋五霸。战国时有七个强大的诸侯，称为战国七雄。（春秋战国都是诸侯争霸的时代。他们为齐桓公、晋文公、秦穆公、宋襄公和楚庄王。战国是七雄征战的时代，他们各据一方，分别是齐、楚、燕、韩、赵、卫、秦七国。）

三字經：中華蒙學經典

Translation:

The first part of Eastern Zhou was called "Spring and Autumn," and the second part was called "Warring States." Five powerful dukes, referred to as the Five Chieftains or Five Hegemonists, dominated the country during the Spring and Autumn period; the Seven Mighty Kingdoms emerged in the Warring States period.

Background information:

The periods of Spring and Autumn and Warring States were a tumultuous phase in Chinese history. As each state tried to gain control of the country and restore the old Chinese kingdom, there were constant civil wars. Among the various states, there were the Five Chieftains and the Seven Mighty Kingdoms. The Five Chieftains in the Spring and Autumn period were the Duke of Qi, the Duke of Jin, the Duke of Chu, the Duke of Qin, and the Duke of Song. The Seven Mighty Kingdoms were those of Qi, Chu, Yan, Han, Zhao, Wei, and Qin. However, while China was divided into smaller competing states politically, intellectual and philosophical activities flourished. Traveling scholars and military strategists moved frequently from region to region to sell their ideas and to counsel rulers.

Chapter 53

Original Text in Simplified Characters:

yíng	qín	shì	shǐ	jiān	bìng
嬴	秦	氏，	始	兼	并。

chuán	èr	shì	chǔ	hàn	zhēng
传	二	世，	楚	汉	争。

Original Text in Traditional Characters:

嬴　秦　氏，　始　兼　并。
傳　二　世，　楚　漢　爭。

Notes:

兼并: to annex

楚汉争: the contention of Chu and Han

Modern Chinese:

秦王嬴政打败了战国七雄的其他六个国家，兼并了他们的领土，统一了中国，建立了秦朝，称为秦始皇。秦始皇是一个暴君，他的皇位传到了第二代，即他的儿子胡亥时，爆发了汉王刘邦和西楚霸王项羽争夺天下之战，从而导致了秦朝的灭亡。

Translation:

King Ying Zheng of Qin, better known as the First Emperor or Qin Shihuang, defeated the rest of the six Kingdoms, gained control of their land, and united China under one state. Qin was a cruel emperor. After his death, his throne was passed on to his son Huhai. The Qin dynasty was overthrown at the onset of the civil war between Liu Bang of Han and Xiang Yu of Chu.

Background information:

The First Emperor of Qin is a controversial character in Chinese history. On the one hand, he was credited with the unification of China, implementing a number of measures that made China strong, including the standardization of written language, currency, weight and measurement systems, and the building of infrastructure. On the other hand, he adopted le-

三字經: 中華蒙學經典

galism as the state philosophy, and imposed harsh taxation and harsh rule on his subjects. He also undertook monumental construction projects to build the Great Wall and his mausoleum, where life-sized terracotta warriors were made to protect his tomb. Both projects took thousands of Chinese lives.

The First Emperor was obsessed with the idea of immortality. He had alchemists make elixirs for him to consume in order to gain long life. He also sent a general with three thousand virgin boys and girls to the east ocean off China to seek elixirs. Shortly after his death, a civil war took place in China and overthrew the Qin dynasty.

The site of terracotta warriors is a major tourism attraction in China today. It is also on the World Heritage list. However, the burial chamber of the First Emperor is intact, as archeologists are still working on the technologies to preserve the artifacts should the tomb be opened.

Chapter 54

Original Text in Simplified Characters:

gāo	zǔ	xīng	hàn	yè	jiàn
高	祖	兴，	汉	业	建。

zhì	xiào	píng	wáng	mǎng	cuàn
至	孝	平，	王	莽	篡。

Original Text in Traditional Characters:

高	祖	興，	漢	業	建。
至	孝	平，	王	莽	篡。

Notes:

高祖: Gaozu, the title of the founding emperor of the Han dynasty

汉: the Han dynasty

兴: to rise

业: cause, enterprise

建: to establish

孝平: Xiaoping, an era name of another Han emperor

王莽: Wang Mang, name

篡: to usurp

Modern Chinese:

汉高祖刘邦打败了项羽建立了西汉王朝，定都西安，到了汉朝的孝平帝时，外戚王莽篡权夺了王位，建立新朝。

Translation:

Liu Bang of Han rose, defeated Xiang Yu, and established the Western Han dynasty with Xi'an as its capital. He was called Emperor Gaozu of Han. Wang Mang usurped the throne during the reign of Emperor Xiaoping, and founded the Xin dynasty.

Background information:

Liu Bang was one of the two peasants in Chinese history who rose to become an emperor. The war between Liu Bang and Xiang Yu, also referred as the "Contention between Liu Bang and Xiang Yu," had many famous historical events that generated materials for operas and literature later. During the famous Dinner at Hongmen （Hongmen Yan 鸿门宴）, Xiang Yu had several opportunities to assassinate Liu Bang to declare himself King; however, he refrained from doing so. *Farewell My Concubine* 霸王別姬 was a classic story in the Beijing opera that's based on the last battle between Liu Bang and Xiang Yu. With the aid of talented military strategist Han Xin, Lu Bang defeated Xiang Yu's army by the bank of the Wu River, and Xiang Yu eventually committed suicide, feeling too responsible for the lives lost, and giving up an opportunity to escape back to his home. Although defeated, Xiang Yu was considered a hero in Chinese history. He was known for his extraordinary bravery, his loyalty to his soldiers and fellow countrymen, as well as the romantic story between him and his concubine Yu Ji.

Wang Mang, who eventually usurped the thrown of Han, was a Confucian scholar. He produced a number of economic reforms, trying to copy the system in the ancient Shang dynasty. However, his reforms failed and caused his Xin dynasty (New dynasty) to collapse into peasant rebellions.

Chapter 55

Original Text in Simplified Characters:

guāng	wǔ	xīng	wéi	dōng	hàn
光	武	兴，	为	东	汉。
sì	bǎi	nián	zhōng	yú	xiàn
四	百	年，	终	于	献。

Original Text in Traditional Characters:

光	武	興，	為	東	漢。
四	百	年，	終	于	獻。

Notes:

光武: Guangwu, an era name of the Han dynasty

终: to end 　　于: at

献: Xian, an era name of the Han dynasty

Modern Chinese:

光武帝刘秀发兵，打败了王莽，建立了东汉王朝，定都洛阳。汉朝又分为西汉和东汉，共持续了四百年，到了汉献帝时灭亡。

Translation:

Liu Xiu of Han defeated Wang Mang and established the Eastern Han dynasty with its capital in Luoyang. He was called Emperor Guangwu of Han. The Han dynasty lasted for four hundred years, divided between Western Han and Eastern Han, and ended with Emperor Xian.

Background information:

The Han dynasty was a prominent era in Chinese history, during which the Silk Road connected the Roman Empire and China, facilitating cultural and economic ex-

changes. The Han emperor sent General Zhang Qian to the West to find foreign allies to defeat the Huns. This endeavor helped open the Silk Road. There were Roman gold coins found in Luoyang, the capital of Eastern Han. Confucianism was restored as an orthodox philosophy during the Han dynasty. There were many technological advances in this period as well. Paper, the compass, and the seismograph, a device to detect earthquakes, were invented during the Han dynasty.

　　　　　　　　三字經: 中華蒙學經典

Chapter 56

Original Text in Simplified Characters:

wèi	shǔ	wú	zhēng	hàn	dǐng
魏	蜀	吴，	争	汉	鼎。

hào	sān	guó	qì	liǎng	jìn
号	三	国，	迄	两	晋。

Original Text in Traditional Characters:

魏	蜀	吳，	爭	漢	鼎。
號	三	國，	迄	兩	晉。

Notes:

魏蜀吴: Wei Shu Wu, the names of the three kingdoms based in different regions in China

争: to contend, to fight over

鼎: tripod symbolizing state power

三国: Three Kingdoms, a historical period in China

Modern Chinese:

汉末时期，曹魏、蜀汉和东吴为了争夺汉朝的江山，互相攻打，形成了三国鼎立的局面。这个时期称为三国，一直持续到两晋。（两晋为东晋和西晋。西晋的开创是因为司马炎兴起，灭了三国，定都于洛阳，后迁都于建康（现在的南京），称为东晋。）

Translation:

At the end of the Han dynasty, there were three kingdoms: Cao Wei, Shu Han, and Eastern Wu, each claiming to be the legitimate successor of the Han dynasty, and fighting to annihilate the other two to control China. This period is called the Three Kingdoms period. It lasted till the Two Jin period, when Sima Yan rose, defeated the Three Kingdoms, and established the Western Jin with its capital in Luoyang. The capital was then moved to Jian Kang, the present Nanjing, at a later time.

Background information:

The Three Kingdoms period was an era in China that provided a background for many interesting characters and stories in Chinese literature and drama. One of the four Chinese classic novels, *Romance of the Three Kingdoms* 三国演义, was based on the historical conflict between the three kingdoms of Wei, Shu, and Wu. The Kingdom of Wei was in the northern part of China, headed by General Cao Cao. General Cao was a high government official in the Eastern Han dynasty. He laid the foundation for his son to later establish the State of Wei in the northern part of China. Cao was not only a military strategist, but also a brilliant poet, although he was often portrayed as a cunning character in fiction and drama. The Kingdom of Shu was in the southwestern part of China, headed by General Liu Bei. In the novel *Romance of the Three Kingdoms,* Liu Bei was portrayed as a benevolent and humble leader who values friendship. The Kingdom of Wu was in the eastern part of China. The founder of the Wu kingdom was Sun Quan. There were many battles during the Three Kingdoms period, among them, the epic battle of Red Cliff, *chi bi zhi zhan* 赤壁之战, was most well known.

三字經: 中華蒙學經典

Chapter 57

Original Text in Simplified Characters:

sòng	qí	jì	liáng	chén	chéng
宋	齐	继，	梁	陈	承。

wéi	nán	cháo	dū	jīn	líng
为	南	朝，	都	金	陵。

Original Text in Traditional Characters:

宋	齊	繼，	梁	陳	承。
為	南	朝，	都	金	陵。

Notes:

继: to continue, to succeed

承: to carry on

南朝: the Southern Dynasties

都: to establish the capital

金陵: Jinling, an old name for the present city of Nanjing

Modern Chinese:

两晋后相继有四个朝代，他们分别为宋朝、齐朝、梁朝、陈朝，统称为南朝，都定都在金陵（今天的南京）。

Translation:

After the two Jin Dynasties, there were four dynasties—Song, Qi, Liang, Chen—together they were called the Southern Dynasties. All had their capitals in Jingling (the present city of Nanjing).

Background information:

Nanjing is one of the four ancient capitals in China. It served as the capital for six dynasties, including the Southern Dynasties of Song, Qi, Liang, and Chen. Nanjing literally means southern capital. It was said that when Emperor Qin, the First Emperor of China, visited Nanjing, his Fengshui soothsayers told him that Nanjing was a place for potential kings. Worried about future competitors, the emperor ordered a river to be dug through the city of Nanjing to "cut off" its possibility for any potential king to rise up. This river is the famous Qinhuai River, which served as a memorable spot for many literary scholars in future generations. Interestingly, none of the dynasties with its capital in Nanjing lasted for long periods of time. During WWII, Japanese troops invaded China in 1937 and committed the infamous Nanjing Massacre, where thousands of innocent civilians were killed. Nanjing was also the capital of the Republic of China after the last dynasty, the Qing dynasty, when Kuomintang, headed by Dr. Sun Yat-san and Chiang Kai-shek, took over China. When the Communist Party, led by Mao Zedong, won the civil war in China, Beijing was chosen as the capital.

Chapter 58

Original Text in Simplified Characters:

běi	yuán	wèi	fēn	dōng	xī
北	元	魏，	分	东	西。

yǔ	wén	zhōu	yǔ	gāo	qí
宇	文	周，	与	高	齐。

三字經: 中華蒙學經典

Original Text in Traditional Characters:

北　元　魏，　分　東　西。
宇　文　周，　與　高　齊。

Notes:

分: to be divided into

宇文周: Yuwen established the Northern Zhou dynasty

与: and

高齐: Gao established the Northern Qi dynasty

Modern Chinese:

与南朝同时存在的是北朝。少数民族鲜卑族的拓跋圭在北方建立魏朝，他改姓元，所以叫元魏。魏朝又分为东魏和西魏，后来高洋灭掉了东魏建立北齐；宇文觉灭掉了西魏建立北周。

Translation:

While the Southern Dynasties had their capitals in Nanjing, there were the Northern Dynasties in northern China at the same time. A minority tribe by the name of Xianbei, led by clan leader Tuoba Gui, established the Wei dynasty. Tuoba Gui changed his name to a Chinese family name Yuan. Therefore, the Wei dynasty was also called Yuan Wei. Wei was divided into Eastern Wei and Western Wei. Later on, Gaoyang defeated Eastern Wei and established Northern Qi; Yuwen Jue defeated Western Wei and established Northern Zhou.

Background information:

The Han Chinese civilization started near the Yellow River valley. There have been many minority ethnic groups in China.

Han is the dominating ethnic group. The northern part of China had been susceptible to the invasion of foreign tribes since the beginning of Chinese history. The reason that several Chinese dynasties had their capitals in southern China was because the emperors were forced to relocate to the south as non-Han tribes controlled northern China. However, when minority tribes invaded and settled in China, they generally became sinicized gradually, eventually adopting the Chinese language and culture, starting interracial marriages, and becoming part of China.

Chapter 59

Original Text in Simplified Characters:

dài	zhì	suí	yì	tǔ	yǔ
迨	至	隋，	一	土	宇。
bù	zài	chuán	shī	tǒng	xù
不	再	传，	失	统	绪。

Original Text in Traditional Characters:

迨	至	隋，	一	土	宇。
不	再	傳，	失	統	緒。

Notes:

迨: to wait until

隋: the Sui dynasty

土: land

宇: heaven

三字經：中華蒙學經典

失: to lose

统: control, ruling

绪: order

Modern Chinese:

等到隋朝时，隋文帝杨坚结束了南北朝，又统一了中国。但是他的皇位传给了儿子杨广之后，由于杨广昏庸残暴，隋朝很快就灭亡了。隋朝的帝位只传了一代就由此而中断。

Translation:

The founding emperor Yang Jian of the Sui dynasty, who was also posthumously titled Sui Wendi, once again united China, ending the Northern and Southern Dynasties situation. However, after Emperor Yang Jian passed his crown to his son Yang Guang, the Sui dynasty reign only survived for one generation. Yang Guang was a tyrannical ruler who brought the Sui dynasty to its demise.

Background information:

After the Eastern Han dynasty, China was divided among various regions due to competing military and political powers. It was not until the Sui dynasty that China was reunited again. Emperor Sui Wendi was most notable for his reunification of China, which laid the foundation for successive dynasties to prosper. The legendary Imperial Examination was initiated during the Sui dynasty. It provided the meritocracy-based government official selection process. The Imperial Examinations lasted till the last dynasty of China, the Qing dynasty. In addition, the Grand Canal also was constructed during the Sui dynasty. It provided convenient transportation between the northern and southern parts of China, making it possible for the goods from the south to be transported to the north. However, the Grand Canal project was also a major factor that caused Emperor Yang Guan's unpopularity, as he used forced labor. The project also contributed to the depletion of the imperial coffers. The Sui dynasty only lasted for two generations.

Chapter 60

Original Text in Simplified Characters:

táng	gāo	zǔ	qǐ	yì	shī
唐	高	祖，	起	义	师。

chú	suí	luàn	chuàng	guó	jī
除	隋	乱，	创	国	基。

Original Text in Traditional Characters:

唐	高	祖，	起	義	師。
除	隋	亂，	創	國	基。

Notes:

唐: the Tang dynasty

起: to raise

义: righteous

师: army

除: to get rid of

乱: chaos

创: to establish　　基: foundation

三字經: 中華蒙學經典

Modern Chinese:

唐高祖李渊，受儿子李世民的劝谏，兴起义兵，推翻了隋帝的统治，平定了隋朝末年的混乱局面，为后来唐朝的江山开创了根基。

Translation:

The first emperor of the Tang dynasty, Tang Gaozu Li Yuan, aided by his Son Li Shimin, led a military revolt and overthrew the Sui dynasty. Tang Gaozu brought peace to the chaotic country, and laid the foundation for a prosperous Tang dynasty.

Background information:

Li Yuan, the first emperor of Tang, was related to the royal family of Sui. Although he was the founding emperor of the Tang dynasty, his son Li Shimin was instrumental in helping him seize the throne from the Sui dynasty. Li Shimin later killed two of his brothers to eliminate the competition for the crown, and inherited the kingdom from his father.

The Tang dynasty was one of the strongest historical periods in China. Tang's territory included part of today's Asian minor. Its capital, Chang'an, served as a metropolitan city of diverse people and culture for the civilized world. Foreign scholars and merchants frequented Chang'an. The exchange of goods and ideas on the Silk Road flourished during this period. A Chinese Buddhist monk by the name of Xuanzang traveled 10,000 miles westward to India and brought back authentic Buddhism scriptures, which were stored in the Big Goose Pagoda in Chang'an later. The famous classic novel *Journey to the West* was based on Xuanzang's pilgrimage.

The development of Chinese poetry was at its zenith in the Tang dynasty. Many famous poets, including Li Bai, were creative artists in this era. Their personal stories intertwined with political figures in the court. Tang poetry has been in the curriculum of Chinese education since then. Chinese children are taught to recite the 1,400-year- old Tang poems till this day.

The Tang dynasty had such an influence on Chinese culture that the Chinatown overseas is called *Tang ren jie* 唐人街 (the street of the Tang people), and overseas Chinese people are sometimes referred to as *Tang ren* 唐人 (the Tang people).

Another interesting fact about the Tang dynasty is that the only woman emperor in

李渊起兵时登坛誓众

Chinese history, Wu Zetian, was a ruler in Tang dynasty. Empress Wu was rather a controversial character. However, during her reign, women had more rights and social status than other dynasties.

三字經: 中華蒙學經典

Chapter 61

Original Text in Simplified Characters:

èr	shí	chuán	sān	bǎi	zài
二	十	传，	三	百	载。

liáng	miè	zhī	guó	nǎi	gǎi
梁	灭	之，	国	乃	改。

Original Text in Traditional Characters:

二	十	傳，	三	百	載。
梁	滅	之，	國	乃	改。

Notes:

传: succession

灭: to extinguish

之: it

乃: then

改: to change

Modern Chinese:

唐朝的皇位传了二十代，一共有近三百年。最后被梁王朱温篡位，结束了唐朝，改国号为"梁"，史称"后梁"。

Translation:

The Tang dynasty lasted for about three hundred years with twenty successions of imperial power. Zhu Wen, founder of the Liang dynasty, usurped the throne and changed the dynasty title to Liang, which was called "Later Liang" in history.

Background information:

In contrast to the prosperity of its earlier stages, the Tang dynasty ended in fragility and strife, as the imperial power dwindled away and various regional governors secured more and more military power and political influence. The era that followed the Tang dynasty was referred to as the Five Dynasties and the Ten Kingdoms, because they were all short-lived, and were relatively insignificant dynasties. Zhu Wen, founder of the Liang dynasty and the first ruler of the Five Dynasties, was a man of poor character, who was an opportunist, ascending to power through ruthless military campaigns. After controlling a teenage puppet Tang emperor for a while, he usurped the throne, and put the Tang emperor, as well as key ministers of the Tang dynasty to death, and established the Liang dynasty. Ironically, Zhu was eventually killed by his son, who was eager to seize the throne for himself.

Chapter 62

Original Text in Simplified Characters:

liáng	táng	jìn	jí	hàn	zhōu
梁	唐	晋，	及	汉	周。
chēng	wǔ	dài	jiē	yǒu	yóu
称	五	代，	皆	有	由。

Original Text in Traditional Characters:

梁	唐	晉，	及	漢	周。
稱	五	代，	皆	有	由。

　　　　　　　　三字經: 中華蒙學經典

Notes:

称: to be called

五代: the Five Dynasties

皆: all

由: reasons

Modern Chinese:

后梁、后唐、后晋、后汉、后周是唐朝之后的五个短暂
的朝代，统称"五代"。他们的建立各有各自的缘由。

Translation:

The Tang dynasty was followed by five short dynasties, namely,
the Later Liang, Later Tang, Later Jin, Later Han, and Later
Zhou. They are called the Five Dynasties. Each had its reasons for rising and falling.

Background information:

There were five short-lived dynasties in the northern part of
China between the Tang and Song dynasties. At the same time,
there were ten kingdoms in the southern part of China. This
was a result of the weakening of imperial power at the end of
the Tang dynasty, whereas various warlords declared themselves emperors. While the ten kingdoms in the south were
relatively stable, the five dynasties in the north were full of
political and military upheaval. A revolving drama of killing,
revenge, and power struggling played out in this historical
scene, all in the name of former legitimate dynasties. That is
why their chosen dynasty names were called the Later Liang,
Tang, Jin, Han, and Zhou.

Chapter 63

Original Text in Simplified Characters:

yán	sòng	xīng	shòu	zhōu	chán
炎	宋	兴，	受	周	禅。

shí	bā	chuán	nán	běi	hùn
十	八	传，	南	北	混。

Original Text in Traditional Characters:

炎	宋	興，	受	周	禪。
十	八	傳，	南	北	混。

Notes:

宋: the Song dynasty

炎: fiery

受: to receive, to accept

禅: abdication

混: to mix

Modern Chinese:

宋太祖赵匡胤陈桥兵变，黄袍加身，接受了后周皇帝的禅让，建立了宋朝。皇位传了十八代，分为北宋和南宋。（北宋定都在汴梁，现在的开封，少数民族金人于 1127 年占领了开封，宋徽宗和儿子宋钦宗投降。宋徽宗的另一个儿子宋高宗和一些贵族南迁，定都杭州，建立了南宋。 蒙古人于 1260 年打败南宋，建立元朝， 又统一了中国。）

三字經：中華蒙學經典

Translation:

Emperor Taizu of the Song dynasty, Zhao Kuangyin, established the Song dynasty as a result of a military coup. He put on the dragon robe and succeeded the Later Zhou dynasty. Song's reign transmitted itself down to eighteen generations. It was divided into the Northern Song and the Southern Song, with Bianliang, the present-day Kaifeng, as its capital in the north, and Hangzhou as its capital in the south.

Background information:

Emperor Zhao Kuangyin came from a martial arts background before he took the throne. Zhao's military takeover at Chenqiao (*Chenqiao bing bian* 陈桥兵变) was less violent than the regular military coups. Although it seemed that Zhao took the throne reluctantly, as his soldiers and generals forced the dragon robe on him after seeing divine signs, the event might have been a well calculated one in advance.

Another famous historical incidence about Emperor Zhao was the story of his skillful persuasion of his generals to give up their military power and retire from government service after the Song dynasty was officially founded (*bei jiu shi bing quan* 杯酒释兵权). Because Zhou took power by force, he was very conscientious of the danger of military power. During his reign, he discouraged military power consolidation, and encouraged the development of arts, literature, science, and technology. As a result, literature in the form of Song poems reached another zenith in Chinese literary history. There were also new styles and development in painting. Imperial examinations were widely spread, which in turn promoted advancement through education. Printing and gun powder were also invented in the Song dynasty. Population increased significantly and economy was prosperous in the Song dynasty. Neo-Confucianism, a form of Confucianism mixed with Buddhist ideals, emerged during the Southern Song dynasty.

The division of the Northern and Southern Song dynasties was the result of a foreign tribe invasion in the northern Chinese border. For years, the Song dynasty kept peace with the minority tribe in the north by paying them annual tribute. However, Jin's people invaded China and conquered Song's capital Kaifeng in 1127, capturing Emperor Song Huizong and his son Qinzong. Another son of the emperor, Song Gaozong, fled to the south, along with some aristocrats and ministers, then established the Southern Song dynasty with its capital in Hangzhou. In 1260, the Mongolians defeated the Southern Song dynasty, and reunited China.

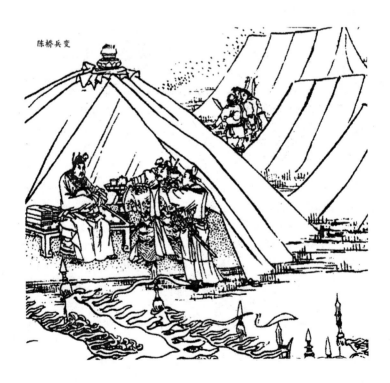

陈桥兵变

三字經: 中華蒙學經典

Chapter 64

Original Text in Simplified Characters:

shí	qī	shǐ	quán	zài	zī
十	七	史,	全	在	兹。

Original Text in Traditional Characters:

十　七　史,　全　在　兹。

Notes:

史: history books

全: all, complete

兹: here

Modern Chinese:

中国的十七部历史书的简介都在这里了。

Translation:

The seventeen official Chinese history books recorded the aforementioned major historic events.

Background information:

The original book of San Zi Jing recorded Chinese history up till the previous chapter, where it stopped at the Southern Song dynasty, because the book itself was written in the Southern Song dynasty. However, San Zi Jing continued to be a popular primer till the late Qing dynasty. Scholars of later generations added verses to the history part of this book to update the narration of history to suit their needs. Chapters 64a-68a and 64b-68b gave two popular versions of the description of history after the Song dynasty. The following are the seventeen history books up to the Song dynasty:

1. Shi Ji, *Records of the Grand Historian,* by Sima Qian of the Han dynasty.

2. Qian Han Shu, *Book of Former Han,* by Ban Gu of the Han dynasty.

3. Hou Han Shu, *Book of Later Han,* by Fan Ye, also referred to as Fan Weizong of the (Liu) Song dynasty.

4. San Guo Zhi, *Records of the Three Kingdoms,* by Chen Shou of the Jin dynasty.

5. Jin Shu, *Book of Jin,* by Fang Xunling of the Tang dynasty.

6. Song Shu, *Book of Song,* by Shen Yue of the Liang dynasty.

7. Qi Shu, *Book of Qi,* by Xiao Zixian of the Liang dynasty.

8. Liang Shu, *Book of Liang,* by Yao Silian of the Later Tang dynasty.

9. Chen Shu, *Book of Chen,* by Yao Silian of the Later Tang dynasty.

10. Bei Wei Shu, *Book of Beiwei,* by Wei Shou of the Northern Qi dynasty.

11. Bei Qi Shu, *Book of Northern Qi,* by Li Baiyao of the Later Tang dynasty.

12. Bei Zhou Shu, *Book of Northern Zhou,* by Linghu Defen of the Later Tang.

13. Sui Shu, *Book of Sui,* by Wei Zheng of the Tang dynasty.

14. Nan Shi, *History of the Southern Dynasties (Song, Qi, Liang, Chen),* by Li Yanshou of the Tang dynasty.

15. Bei Shi, *History of the Northern Dynasties (Wei, Qi, Zhou, Sui),* by Li Yanshou of the Tang dynasty.

16. Tang Shu, *Book of Tang,* by Song Qi and Ouyang Xiu of the Song dynasty.

三字經: 中華蒙學經典

17. Wu Dai Shi, *History of the Five Dynasties* by Ouyang Xiu of the Song dynasty.

Chapter 64a*[1]

Original Text in Simplified Characters:

liáo	yǔ	jīn	dì	hào	fēn
辽	与	金，	帝	号	纷，

dài	miè	liáo	sòng	yóu	cún
迨	灭	辽，	宋	犹	存。

Original Text in Traditional Characters:

遼	與	金，	帝	號	紛，
迨	滅	遼，	宋	猶	存。

Notes:

辽: the Liao dynasty

金: the Jin dynasty

帝号: kings' era names

纷: to tangle

犹: still

存: existing

Modern Chinese:

南宋时期，少数民族契丹人在北方建立了辽国。女真族人建立了金国。他们都各自称帝。当金国打败辽国时，南宋依然存在。

The original verses in Chapters 64a-68a are records of history after the Song dynasty. They are written by Wang Xiang 王相, a Qing dynasty scholar.

三字經: 中華蒙學經典

Translation:

At the end of the Southern Song dynasty, the Khitans established the Liao dynasty in the north, and the Jurchens established the Jin dynasty, both ethnic tribes had their emperors. Later the Jurchens conquered the Liao dynasty in the north, and at the same time, the Southern song dynasty survived in the south.

Background information:

The Khitans and the Jurchens were foreign tribes in northern China. Throughout history, they either invaded China or became a tributary of various dynasties. Therefore, the Chinese majority referred to them as ethnic groups. The Khitans were related to tribes of today's Mongolians, and the Jurchens were related to tribes of today's Manchurians. The Jurchens conquered China in the Qing dynasty. When they conquered China, they adopted many aspects of Chinese culture, including Chinese language and their bureaucratic system.

Chapter 65a

Original Text in Simplified Characters:

zhì	yuán	xīng	jīn	xù	xiē
至	元	兴，	金	绪	歇，
yǒu	sòng	shì	yì	tóng	miè
有	宋	世，	一	同	灭。

Original Text in Traditional Characters:

至	元	興，	金	緒	歇，
有	宋	世，	一	同	滅。

Notes:

元: the Yuan dynasty

金绪: the order of the Jin dynasty

歇: to rest

宋世: Song dynasty's kingdom

一同灭: to extinguish all together

Modern Chinese:

等到元朝兴起，蒙古人统一了中国，打败了金国，也一同歼灭了南宋。

Translation:

The Yuan dynasty was founded by the Mongols, who defeated the Jin dynasty as well as the Southern Song dynasty, and reunited China.

Background information:

The founding emperor of the Yuan dynasty was Kublai Khan, grandson of Genghis Khan. During the Yuan dynasty, many foreigners were favored at the imperial court, while the Han Chinese were discriminated against. Under the Mongol empire, the Silk Road was safe to travel again. Marco Polo came to China during the Yuan dynasty. He stayed in China for over twenty years, gaining much favor with Kublai Khan and serving at his court. His book *The Travels of Marco Polo* recorded many things he saw in China, including the usage of paper currency, coal, and postal systems, none of which were in existence in Europe at that time. Therefore, his European peers thought he contrived these fantacies.

During the Yuan dynasty, the imperial examinations were suspended. Chinese scholars used their talent to write plays

三字經: 中華蒙學經典

using vernacular language for mass entertainment. Because of the discouragement of using classical language and the influence of the Mongolian language during the Yuan dynasty, Chinese grammar changed to a large extent.

Chapter 66a

Original Text in Simplified Characters:

bìng	zhōng	guó	jiān	róng	dí
并	中	国，	兼	戎	翟，
jiǔ	shí	nián	guó	zuò	fèi
九	十	年，	国	祚	废。

Original Text in Traditional Characters:

并	中	國，	兼	戎	翟，
九	十	年，	國	祚	廢。

Notes:

并: to annex

兼: to occupy, annex

戎: barbarian tribes in the west of ancient China

翟: barbarian tribes

祚: the throne

废: to waste

Modern Chinese:

蒙古人统治了中国的中原及周边地区的许多少数民族，
在持续了九十年后也灭亡了。

Translation:

The Mongols governed China and its surrounding tributary minority people groups. Their reign ended after 90 years.

Background information:

元太祖成吉思汗像

Although the Mongol empire was massive and powerful, their rule in China was not popular. Mongolian culture was very different from Chinese culture, one being nomadic and the other being domestic and agricultural. There was a time that Kublai Khan intended to convert the northern Chinese fields to pastures. As Mongols favored foreigners rather than the Chinese during the Yuan dynasty, there was much resentment among the Chinese. Eventually, the Chinese rebelled and overthrew the Mongol rule.

Chapter 67a

Original Text in Simplified Characters:

míng	tài	zǔ	jiǔ	qīn	shī
明	太	祖，	久	亲	师，
chuán	jiàn	wén	fāng	sì	sì
传	建	文，	方	四	祀。

Original Text in Traditional Characters:

明　太　祖，　久　親　師，
傳　建　文，　方　四　祀。

Notes:

明: the Ming dynasty

亲师: to lead the army by himself

传: to transmit

方: only

祀: sacrificial offerings on behalf of the country

Modern Chinese:

明太祖朱元璋亲自带兵南征北战十八年，打败了元朝，
建立了明朝。他的皇位传给了孙子朱允炆，史称"建文
帝"，只当了四年的皇帝就被推翻。

Translation:

Zhu Yuanzhang, also referred to as Ming Taizu, was the
founding emperor of the Ming dynasty. He led military campaigns for eighteen years, defeated the Yuan dynasty, and established the Ming dynasty. He transmitted the throne to his
grandson Zhu Yunwen, also referred to as Emperor Jianwen,
whose rule only lasted for four years.

Background information:

Emperor Zhu Yuanzhang rose from a peasant family to become the founding emperor of Ming during the end of the
Yuan dynasty, when there was much natural and manmade
turmoil in China. Because of his peasant background, Zhu's
policy toward the poor and the masses was benevolent. How-

ever, he was constantly suspicious and paranoid of conspiracy against him. He created a secret service branch of government, which spied on government officials and the society in general, and reported directly to him.

The Ming dynasty was one of the leading civilizations in the world among established nations. The Great Wall went through major reconstruction during the Ming dynasty. General Zheng He took seven sea expeditions, visiting countries as far as the Middle East and Africa. Zhen He's fleet of treasure boats were much larger than its contemporary European ships. The Jesuit missionaries, headed by Matteo Ricci, came to China, learned the Chinese language, and served as important agents in transmitting ideas between the East and the West. On the one hand, they introduced China and classical Chinese philosophy to Europe, and they also confirmed Marco Polo's "Cathy" was China; on the other hand, they brought western mathematics and other scientific ideas to China. The Jesuits introduced western cartography and the calendar system to the Chinese as well.

Literature in the form of novels written in the vernacular language became a popular genre in the Ming dynasty. Several classic novels, including *Journey to the West*, *The Outlaws of the Marsh*, and *The Three Kingdoms*, were written during the Ming dynasty.

Chapter 68a

Original Text in Simplified Characters:

qiān	běi	jīng	yǒng	lè	sì
迁	北	京，	永	乐	嗣，
dài	chóng	zhēn	méi	shān	shì
迨	崇	祯，	煤	山	逝。

三字經: 中華蒙學經典

Original Text in Traditional Characters:

遷　北　京，　永　樂　嗣，
迨　崇　禎，　煤　山　逝。

Notes:

嗣: to succeed

逝: to pass away, to die

Modern Chinese:

明成祖永乐皇帝时，又把国都迁到北京，明朝的最后一个皇帝是崇祯皇帝。他在位时农民起义军李自成的部队攻入北京，崇祯帝在煤山自缢，明朝结束。

Translation:

During Emperor Ming Chengzu Yongle's reign, the capital of Ming was moved to Beijing. The last emperor of Ming was Emperor Chongzhen. The peasant rebellion led by Li Zicheng took place at the end of Ming. When Li's army entered Beijing, Emperor Chongzhen committed suicide at Meishan, which signaled the ending of the Ming dynasty.

Background information:

Emperor Ming Chengzu Yongle's relocation of the capital from Nanjing to Beijing was the result of the internal conflict within the imperial family. Yongle constructed the Forbidden City in Beijing as the Imperial Palace. During his reign, Yongle also commissioned the monumental scholarly work of the *Yongle Encyclopedia*. At the end of the Ming dynasty, eunuchs became a strong political force in the imperial palace. The eunuchs led by Wei Zhongxian 魏忠贤 held power. They abused imperial power for personal gains. Engaging in bitter struggles with other imperial officials, the eunuchs eventually contributed to the downfall of the Ming dynasty.

The peasant rebellion lead by Li Zicheng was also instrumental in terminating the Ming dynasty. While Ming's army was busy combating the Manchurian invasion in the north, Li Zicheng, a peasant by birth, gathered a peasant army and rebelled against the Ming government. They killed numerous officials, took properties and goods from the wealthy and gave them to the poor. Li's revolution eventually was quelled down by the Manchurian army, who took over China at the fall of the Ming dynasty.

Chapter 64b**

Original Text in Simplified Characters:

liáo	yǔ	jīn	jiē	chēng	dì
辽	与	金，	皆	称	帝。

yuán	miè	jīn	jué	sòng	shì
元	灭	金，	绝	宋	世。

Original Text in Traditional Characters:

遼	與	金，	皆	稱	帝。
元	滅	金，	絕	宋	世。

**Chapters 64b-68b are another example of the description of history after the Song dynasty. They were written by He Xingsi 贺兴思, a Qing dynasty scholar. He Xingsi's annotation of San Zi Jing was based on a former Qing scholar Wang Xiang's version. He updated the history part of the book, which also became a popular classic version of San Zi Jing.*

Notes:

皆: all

称帝: to be entitled emperors

绝: to end

宋世: Song dynasty's ruling

Modern Chinese:

两个少数民族，契丹人（即辽人）与女真人（也称金人），占领中国北方后都各称帝，建立了辽国和金国。金国灭掉了辽国，而蒙古人又灭掉了金国和南宋，统一了中国。

Translation:

Two minority tribes, the Liao, also known as the Khitans, and the Jurchens, also referred to as Jin, conquered the northern part of China and established the Liao dynasty and the Jin dynasty. Jin defeated Liao ultimately. The Mongols in turn defeated Jin and the Southern Song dynasty, reuniting China.

Background information:

The Khitans and the Jurchens were two foreign tribes in northern China. When they conquered northern China, the Chinese emperor of Song reestablished the Southern Song dynasty and ruled southern China. The Mongols eventually defeated both the Southern Song dynasty and the Jurchens, who had defeated the Khitans earlier, annexing China into the Mongolian empire.

Chapter 65b

Original Text in Simplified Characters:

lì	zhōng	guó	jiān	róng	dí
莅	中	国,	兼	戎	狄。

jiǔ	shí	nián	guó	zuò	fèi
九	十	年,	国	祚	废。

Original Text in Traditional Characters:

莅	中	国,	兼	戎	狄。
九	十	年,	国	祚	废。

Notes:

莅: to be present, to arrive

Modern Chinese:

元朝统治了中国以及周边许多少数民族地区，在持续了约九十年后，统治权就灭亡了。

Translation:

See 66a.

Background information:

See 66a.

三字經: 中華蒙學經典

Chapter 66b

Original Text in Simplified Characters:

tài	zǔ	xīng	guó	dà	míng
太	祖	兴，	国	大	明。

hào	hóng	wǔ	dōu	jīn	líng
号	洪	武，	都	金	陵。

Original Text in Traditional Characters:

太	祖	興，	國	大	明。
號	洪	武，	都	金	陵。

Notes:

太祖: Taizu, the founding emperor of Ming

国: dynasty

洪武: Hongwu, era name

Modern Chinese:

明太祖朱元璋兴兵打败了元朝的统治，建立了明朝，国号大明。他的年号叫洪武，定都在金陵（现在的南京）。

Translation:

Emperor Ming Taizu, Zhu Yuanzhang, defeated the rule of the Yuan dynasty and established the Ming dynasty, which was also called the Big Ming. Emperor Zhu's reign was titled Hongwu, and its capital was in Jinling (the present city of Nanjing).

Background information:

The names of new dynasties were changed when new families took over as rulers, where the crown became hereditary within the same family along the patriarchic line. Each emperor also chose a name, called the "era name," for his reigning period. There could be several era names within the same dynasty. Sometimes the emperors were also referred to by their era names. Emperor Zhu led the military campaigns for years before he eventually defeated the Yuan dynasty. His chosen era name was Hongwu, meaning, "vast military," indicating his inclination for military power.

明太祖朱元璋像

Chapter 67b

Original Text in Simplified Characters:

dài	chéng	zǔ	qiān	yàn	jīng
迨	成	祖,	迁	燕	京。

shí	liù	shì	zhì	chóng	zhēn
十	六	世,	至	崇	祯。

Original Text in Traditional Characters:

迨　成　祖,　遷　燕　京。

十　六　世,　至　崇　禎。

Notes:

燕京: Yanjing, the present Beijing

世: generations

Modern Chinese:

等到明成祖时，迁都到北京。明朝传了十六代，最后一个皇帝是崇祯。

Translation:

During Emperor Ming Chengzu's era, the capital was moved to Beijing. The Ming dynasty had sixteen imperial successions, and the last emperor was Chongzhen.

Background information:

Emperor Chengzu was the fourth son of the founding emperor of Ming, Zhu Yuangzhang. He was given a princedom near Yanjing, the present-day Beijing. After Zhu's oldest son, the crowned prince, died, the crown was passed to his son, Emperor Jianwen. However, Ming Chengzu usurped his cousin's throne and became the emperor himself. He also relocated the capital from Nanjing to Beijing, where he had a strong military base. Emperor Chengzu's era name was Yongle. During his reign, China reached another height of prosperity.

Chapter 68b

Original Text in Simplified Characters:

quán	yān	sì	kòu	rú	lín
权	阉	肆，	寇	如	林。

zhì	lǐ	chuǎng	shén	qì	fén
至	李	闯,	神	器	焚。

Original Text in Traditional Characters:

權	閹	肆,	寇	如	林。
至	李	闖,	神	器	焚。

Notes:

权: power

阉: eunuchs

肆: unbridled

寇: bandits

如林: like forest

李闯: Dashing Li the King

神器: imperial sacrificial vessels

焚: to be burnt

Modern Chinese:

明朝的末年宦官当权极为嚣张，社会上强盗四起，如麻如林。农民起义领袖李闯王李自成率兵攻占了北京，毁掉了明朝的国家。

Translation:

At the end of the Ming dynasty, the power of eunuchs was unbridled and there were bandits everywhere in the society. Li Zicheng, also titled Dashing Li the King, led a peasant rebellion, arrived in Beijing. His troops looted and burned many places in Beijing, including the imperial palace.

Background information:

Eunuchs were a unique culture in the imperial China. While some eunuchs were from poor families, others were self-castrated to render service in the imperial palace. There were several times in Chinese history when the eunuchs became a strong political force that affected the course of history, and the end of the Ming dynasty was one of them. The eunuchs were more powerful than the government officials in the late Ming dynasty, with Wei Zhongxian as the head of the eunuchs. He took the title "Nine Thousand Years," implying only the emperor, the ten thousand years, was above him. The contention between the eunuchs and the Confucian scholars caused the government to be very weak during the late Ming dynasty. Bandits abounded and the Chinese society was in a state of chaos. Li Zicheng took advantage of the unstable political situation, and easily gathered the famished peasants for a rebellion, which led to the downfall of Ming.

Chapter 69b

Original Text in Simplified Characters:

qīng	tài	zǔ	yīng	jǐng	mìng
清	太	祖，	膺	景	命。
jìng	sì	fāng	kè	dà	dìng
靖	四	方，	克	大	定。

Original Text in Traditional Characters:

清	太	祖，	膺	景	命。
靖	四	方，	克	大	定。

Notes:

膺: to receive

景: situation

命: destiny

靖: to bring about peace, to pacify

四方: all four directions

克: to overcome

定: stability

Modern Chinese:

清太祖努尔哈赤，顺应天时机遇，入关打败李自成建立
了清朝，统一了中国，安抚四方，建立了安定的新朝代。

Translation:

Emperor Qing Taizu, Nurhaci, came into China from Man-
churia, defeated Li Zicheng, and founded the Qing dynasty
with ordained timing. He established peace and stability all
over China again.

Background information:

The Qing dynasty was the second dynasty in Chinese history
when non-Han people established rule. Nurhaci and his descendents who became successive emperors in the Qing dynasty were ethnic Manchurian. They had their own language
and customs. They had been fighting the Chinese army in
northeast China. However, when the peasant revolt led by Li
Zicheng took over Beijing and forced the Ming emperor to
commit suicide, the Ming general Wu Sangui decided to sur-
render to the Manchurians, using their power to defeat Li
Zicheng. Nurhaci and his sons all learned Chinese language
and culture. When they became emperors, they ordered Chi-

三字經: 中華蒙學經典

nese men to cut their hair but keep the pigtails, which was widely resisted in China. However, they did preserve many other aspects of Chinese culture.

Chapter 69

Original Text in Simplified Characters:

niàn	èr	shǐ	quán	zài	zī
廿	二	史，	全	在	兹。

zài	zhì	luàn	zhī	xīng	shuāi
载	治	乱，	知	兴	衰。

Original Text in Traditional Characters:

廿	二	史，	全	在	兹。
載	治	亂，	知	興	衰。

Notes:

廿: twenty

兹: this

载: to record

兴衰: rise and decline

Modern Chinese:

二十二史是二十二本中国史书，它们记载了中国从三皇五帝到明末清初各个朝代兴盛和衰乱的历史，使读者了解历史上各时期兴衰的原由。

Translation:

There were twenty-two history books containing the official history of China, recording the major historical events and the rise and fall of each dynasty from the Three Sovereigns and Five Kings to the end of the Ming dynasty and the beginning of the Qing dynasty. Readers may learn from history and know the reasons for the prosperity and subsequent decline of each era.

Background information:

The twenty-two historical books are official records of Chinese history. They are the seventeen history books in Chapter 64 plus the following five:

18. Song Shi, *History of Song*, by Tuo Tuo, Toktoghan, of the Yuan dynasty.
19. Liao Shi, *History of Liao*, by Tuo Tuo, Toktoghan, of the Yuan dynasty.
20. Jin Shi, *History of Jin*, by Tuo Tuo, Toktoghan, of the Yuan dynasty.
21. Yuan Shi, *History of Yuan*, by Song Lian of the Ming dynasty.
22. Ming Shi, *History of Ming* by Zhang Tingyu of the Qing dynasty.

三字經: 中華蒙學經典

Chapter 70

Original Text in Simplified Characters:

dú	shǐ	shū	kǎo	shí	lù
读	史	书，	考	实	录。

tōng	gǔ	jīn	ruò	qīn	mù
通	古	今，	若	亲	目。

Original Text in Traditional Characters:

讀	史	書，	考	實	錄。
通	古	今，	若	親	目。

Notes:

实: authentic, true

录: record

通: to understand

古今: the past and the present, history

亲: in person, one's own

目: eyes, to look

Modern Chinese:

研读历史的人，要考证查阅历代王朝的真实记录，这样就可以透彻了解从古到今的历史，仿佛自己亲眼看见一样。

Translation:

When the students study history, they need to examine the official annals of each dynasty so as to gain a thorough understanding of the authentic history from the past to the present, and therefore, to learn about the past vicariously.

Background information:

There are commissioned historians in each dynasty to record the historical events as well as the deeds and sayings of Chinese emperors. Emperors were not allowed to look at the record of their reign until the reign was over. Each emperor was to study the history of past generations and to learn from it. The study of history has always been important in Chinese culture.

Chapter 71

Original Text in Simplified Characters:

kǒu	ér	sòng	xīn	ér	wéi
口	而	诵，	心	而	惟。

zhāo	yú	sī	xī	yú	sī
朝	于	斯，	夕	于	斯。

Original Text in Traditional Characters:

口　而　誦，　心　而　惟。
朝　于　斯，　夕　于　斯。

Notes:

口: mouth

诵: to recite

心: heart

惟: to think
朝: morning
于: at
斯: this
夕: evening

Modern Chinese:

读书学习的时候，方法很重要，既要大声朗读背诵， 又
要在心里默默反思理解书的内容。早上要这样学，晚上
也要这样学，不可以间断。

Translation:

When the students engage in learning, it is very important to
pay attention to the reading method. They should not only
read out loud and recite the text, but also try to comprehend it
with silent reflection and careful analysis. They should study
like this consistently in the morning as well as in the evening,
so as not to be interrupted or give up at any time.

Background information:

Reading out loud and in recitation is a popular learning strategy in Chinese education. Students are commended to memorize a large amount of information by this method. In traditional Chinese education settings, the students have an infor-
mal reading-aloud session in the morning when they would
read aloud any subject matter repetitiously to memorize them.
Modern educational specialists also confirm that reading
aloud is a good learning strategy.

Part Four

(Chpaters 72-93)

Examples of Chinese Super Heroes

Chapter 72

Original Text in Simplified Characters:

xī	zhòng	ní	shī	xiàng	tuó
昔	仲	尼，	师	项	橐。

gǔ	shèng	xián	shàng	qín	xué
古	圣	贤，	尚	勤	学。

Original Text in Traditional Characters:

昔	仲	尼，	師	項	橐。
古	聖	賢，	尚	勤	學。

Notes:

仲尼: Zhongni, another name for Confucius

师: to be taught

项橐: Xiang Tuo

圣贤: holy and wise, sages and wises men

尚: to esteem, to value

勤: diligent

Modern Chinese:

从前，孔子不耻下问，向七岁的小神童项橐求教。古代的圣贤尚且如此，勤学好问，那么普通人更应该像孔子一样，努力学习了。

Translation:

In the past, Confucius was very humble to regard a seven-year-old child prodigy by the name of Xiang Tuo as his teacher. Even though already regarded as sages and wise men of great learning, people like Confucius still studied and inquired about knowledge diligently. Ordinary students should learn from them, and study hard.

Background information:

The following chapters use various illustrations to teach the students to study hard. Confucius was the grand master of learning. Not only did he have many wise sayings about how to study, he himself set an example of being a humble student, including learning from Xiang Tuo, a child prodigy. One of the stories recorded the encounter of Confucius and Xiang Tuo. One day, when Xiang Tuo was playing on the road, Confucius and his disciples' cart approached him. Xiang Tuo piled some rocks in a circle around himself and sat there. Confucius' disciples were upset, and questioned him why he did not move and let the cart go by. Xiang Tuo replied, "When a cart approaches a city, the cart should always go around the city. Have you heard that a city should be removed so that the cart can go through?" Confucius was very impressed with the child. It was said that Confucius visited Xiang Tuo's parents and stayed with them to observe and learn from Xiang Tuo.

Chapter 73

Original Text in Simplified Characters:

zhào	zhōng	lìng	dú	lǔ	lún
赵	中	令，	读	鲁	论。

bǐ	jì	shì	xué	qiě	qín
彼	既	仕，	学	且	勤。

三字經: 中華蒙學經典

Original Text in Traditional Characters:

趙　中　令，　讀　魯　論。
彼　既　仕，　學　且　勤。

Notes:

趙中令: Grand Secretary Zhao

魯: Lu, the region where Confucius is from, the present Shangdong province

論: *The Analects of Confucius*

仕: government official

且: also, in addition to

Modern Chinese:

宋朝的赵普曾任中书令和宰相。他好读《论语》，而且用《论语》里的知识帮助宋太祖、宋太宗两位皇帝治理天下。象赵普这样已当上宰相的人，还勤奋地学习，更何况普通人呢？

Translation:

Zhao Pu was Grand Secretary and Prime Minister in the Song dynasty. He liked to read the *Analects of Confucius*, furthermore, he was able to use what he learned in the book to help Emperors Taizu and Taizong govern the country. Although Zhao Pu was already a high government official, he continued to be very diligent in his studies. Common students should likewise study diligently.

Background information:

Zhao Pu first served as Grand Secretary, then as Prime Minister in the Song dynasty. It was said that he was very fond of

The Analects of Confucius and loved to read it. Because he first served under Emperor Taizu, then served under Emperor

Taizong, it was said that he used "half of the *Analects* to govern the country with each emperor, *bian bu lun yu zhi tian xia* 半部论语治天下."

Chapter 74

Original Text in Simplified Characters:

pī	pú	biān	xuē	zhú	jiǎn
披	蒲	编，	削	竹	简。
bǐ	wú	shū	qiě	zhī	miǎn
彼	无	书，	且	知	勉。

Original Text in Traditional Characters:

披　蒲　編，　削　竹　簡。
彼　無　書，　且　知　勉。

Notes:

披: to split open

蒲: cattail grass

編: to weave

削: to pare with a knife

竹簡: bamboo slips

彼: they

勉: to strive, to exert, to make effort

Modern Chinese:

西汉时有个牧羊人叫路温舒，用蒲草编成席子，把借来
的《尚书》抄在上面学习；另一个赶猪人叫公孙弘，把
竹子削成竹简，借来《春秋》一书，抄在竹简上学习。
他们两人都没有钱买书，却知道想办法看书，努力学习。

Translation:

A shepherd by the name of Lu Wenshu in the Western Han
dynasty liked to study. He made a scroll out of cattail grass,
borrowed *The Book of History* and copied the entire book on it
to study. Another man by the name of Gong Sunhong made a
living by raising pigs for others. Gong Sunhong made a scroll
out of bamboo, borrowed the book *The Spring and Autumn
Annals*, and copied the book on it to study. Both individuals
were too poor to afford books, but they created ways to read
and learn.

Background information:

Books were expensive commodities in early China. Before paper was invented in the Han dynasty, books were written on silk or bamboo strips. They were expensive because each book had to be handwritten. Only the wealthy could afford books. The invention and use of printing technology in the Song dynasty made books more accessible for the common people.

The above stories mentioned both people copied the books they borrowed to make their own books to study, regardless of copyright issues. Issues regarding copyright and intellectual property, especially the copyright of literature, were not very important in traditional Chinese history. Citations of the classics without giving the credits to the sources were expected and encouraged, because the implication was that any learned people should have known the sources. As a result of their studies, both individuals from the above stories eventually became high officials.

Chapter 75

Original Text in Simplified Characters:

tóu	xuán	liáng	zhuī	cì	gǔ
头	悬	梁，	锥	刺	股。
bǐ	bù	jiào	zì	qín	kǔ
彼	不	教，	自	勤	苦。

Original Text in Traditional Characters:

頭	懸	梁，	錐	刺	股。
彼	不	教，	自	勤	苦。

三字經: 中華蒙學經典

Notes:

头: head

悬: to hang

梁: roof beam

锥: awl

刺: to prick

股: thigh

Modern Chinese:

晋朝一个叫孙敬的人，读书时为了避免打瞌睡，用绳子把头发系在头顶的房梁上；战国时有一个叫苏秦的人，也是为了避免读书时打瞌睡，就用锥子去刺自己的大腿。他们两个人这样做都不是别人教的，而是自己勤奋用功，在读书时敢于吃苦。

Translation:

A person by the name of Sun Jing in the Jin dynasty used a rope to pull his hair up from the roof beam to prevent himself from falling asleep during his studies. Another person in the Warring States period, by the name of Su Qin, used an awl to prick his thigh to wake himself up when he fell asleep during his studies. No one taught these men to do so; they were motivated to learn on their own.

Background information:

Chinese men had long hair throughout history. Therefore, it was possible for Sun Jing to tie his hair with a rope to the roof beam. Both men in this story inflicted upon themselves physical pain in order to study hard. They both became high officials later due to their motivation and hard work. Since time is limited and man cannot create extra time, many people try to sleep less in order to achieve more. When the Jesuit missionaries came to China to evangelize, they had to learn Chinese, which was not an easy task. They chose to give up sleep in order to learn it fast. James Legge, the prolific British sinologist who translated most of classic Chinese works into English, also stole time from his sleep to accomplish his monumental translation project. Self-discipline is a universal characteristic for people who are determined to achieve more.

Chapter 76

Original Text in Simplified Characters:

rú	náng	yíng	rú	yìng	xuě
如	囊	萤,	如	映	雪。
jiā	suī	pín	xué	bù	chuò
家	虽	贫,	学	不	辍。

Original Text in Traditional Characters:

如	囊	螢,	如	映	雪。
家	雖	貧,	學	不	輟。

Notes:
囊: to bag

萤: firefly

映: to reflect

雪: snow

家: family

贫: poor

辍: to stop

Modern Chinese:

晋朝有一个叫车胤的人，家里贫穷没有钱点油灯，晚上
没法看书，就捉来萤火虫放在网袋里，借着它们的光看
书。另外一个叫孙康的人，也是没有钱买油灯，冬天的
晚上就在户外借着雪地的反光来念书。虽然他们两人都
是家里贫穷，却不因此放弃学习。

Translation:

A poor man called Che Yin in the Jin dynasty did not have
money to buy an oil lamp, so he caught fireflies and put them
in a net to use as light to read at night. Another poor man by
the name of Sun Kang did not have money for the oil lamp,
either, so in the winter time, he read by the light reflected
from the snow outside in the evenings. Both were from poor
families, yet they did not stop learning.

Background information:

The above two people overcame their poverty and were determined to learn. Because of the influence of Confucian
thought and the process of imperial examinations, education
has always been an important element in Chinese culture.
Education is the key to success. Anyone can be promoted
through hard work in learning. Education in Chinese culture is
always portrayed as hard work rather than a fun activity.
"Study hard" is translated as *ke ku xue xi* 刻苦学习, literally,
carving/penetrating, bitterness, learn, practice. A proverb says,
"Diligence is the shortcut to the mountain of books; Bitterness is the boat to float in the boundless ocean of studies, *shu
shan you lu qin wei jing, xue hai wu ya ku zuo zhou* 书山有路勤为径,

学海无涯苦做舟." The students in Chinese culture have always been taught that learning requires hard work, and they were to follow examples of Che Yin and Sun Kang. Students of later generations do not have to read by firefly's light and snow reflection, as their situations are much better than the poor Che Yin and Sun Kang, but they need to be equally determined and motivated in learning.

Chapter 77

Original Text in Simplified Characters:

rú	fù	xīn	rú	guà	jiǎo
如	负	薪，	如	挂	角。

shēn	suī	láo	yóu	kǔ	zhuō
身	虽	劳，	犹	苦	卓。

Original Text in Traditional Characters:

如	員	薪，	如	挂	角。
身	雖	勞，	猶	苦	卓。

Notes:

负: to carry 薪: firewood

挂: to hang 角: horn

身: body, physically

劳: to labor, to toil

犹: yet

卓: exceptional, outstanding, extraordinary

三字經: 中華蒙學經典

Modern Chinese:

汉朝有个叫朱买臣的人，是一个砍柴郎。但是他很好学，
常常在背柴的路上，一边走路，一边看书；隋朝有个叫
叫李密的人，是一个放牛郎，他也是好学的榜样，常常
在放牛时把书挂在牛角上，骑着牛看书，想办法学习。
他们两个人虽然做的都是很辛苦的体力劳动，但是他们
却克服困难，刻苦学习，成为卓越的榜样。

Translation:

There was a studious man by the name of Zhu Maichen in the
Han dynasty, who made a living by gathering firewood. He
would often read on the road while he was walking and carry-
ing the firewood on his back. Another exemplary diligent
person was Li Mi in the Sui dynasty, who made a living by
tending cows. He would hang the books on the cow's horn,
and read while he was riding the cow. Both men had to do
manual labor and endure physical hardship, yet they overcame
difficulties and found ways to study in the most exceptional
ways.

Background information:

The two men in the above story both became government
officials as a result of their hard work in study. The classic
"Chinese Dream" was that a person from a lowly background
would study extraordinarily diligently, overcome many difficulties to become a scholar, and rise to be a high-ranking government official. Chinese officials in history were usually
scholar-officials, as they had to pass the imperial examinations
dominated by Confucian philosophy to become civil servants.

Traditional Confucian thought despised manual labor and
upheld intellectual work. A Chinese proverb says, "Everything
else is not worth doing; reading is the only noble endeavor.
wan ban jie xia pin, wei you du shu gao 万般皆下品，唯有读书高."

Another one says, "Those who use their heads rule, and those who use their hands are ruled by others. *lao xin zhe zhi ren, lao li zhe zhi yu ren* 劳心者治人，劳力者治与人." It is believed that "There are beautiful women in books, and there are golden houses in books as well, *shu zhong zi you yan ru yu, shu zhong zi you huang jin wu* 书中自有颜如玉，书中自有黄金屋," implying that reading and studying is the only way for social advancement and prosperity in life.

Chapter 78

Original Text in Simplified Characters:

sū	lǎo	quán	èr	shí	qī
苏	老	泉，	二	十	七。

shǐ	fā	fèn	dú	shū	jí
始	发	愤，	读	书	籍。

Original Text in Traditional Characters:

蘇	老	泉，	二	十	七。
始	發	憤，	讀	書	籍。

Notes:

二十七: twenty-seven years old

发愤: to make a firm resolution

书籍: books

Modern Chinese:

宋朝时的文学家苏洵，号老泉，是苏东坡的父亲。他大器晚成，二十七岁时才开始发奋读书。

Translation:

A scholar in the Song dynasty by the name of Su Xun, also referred to as Su Laoquan, was the father of Su Dongpo, the famous poet. He did not begin to study hard until he was 27 years old, upon which time he read voraciously and became an accomplished scholar.

Background information:

Even though Su Xun wasted time in his youth and did not study hard, he nevertheless mended his erroneous ways and

started to study seriously when he was 27 years old. Su Xun had two sons, Su Zhe and Su Shi, the latter often being referred to as Su Dongpo. Together they were called the Three Sus. Su Xun and his two sons all became well known scholars in the Song dynasty. The oldest son, Su Dongpo, was best known for his poetry, prose, calligraphy, and painting.

Chapter 79

Original Text in Simplified Characters:

bǐ	jì	lǎo	yóu	huǐ	chí
彼	既	老，	犹	悔	迟。

ěr	xiǎo	shēng	yí	zǎo	sī
尔	小	生，	宜	早	思。

Original Text in Traditional Characters:

彼	既	老，	猶	悔	遲。
爾	小	生，	宜	早	思。

Notes:

悔: to regret

迟: late

小生: young people

宜: should, ought to

早: early

思: to think

Modern Chinese:

苏老泉他已经年纪这么大了，还后悔自己开始努力学习得太晚了，你们这些年轻的学生应该提早深思觉悟，努力读书。

Translation:

Su Laoquan was quite old to repent for his late start; nevertheless, he realized the need to study. You young people should consider these things as early as possible, and study diligently.

Background information:
Traditional Chinese children's education started at eight. Nowadays, children go to school at age six. Chinese children are taught not to waste time, but to devote themselves to study whole-heartedly and diligently. They were taught that knowledge is the best kind of treasure that one can carry with him whenever he goes, and that thieves cannot steal. Most Chinese children are not expected to do chores at home. Their sole responsibility is to study. Current Chinese educational philosophy advocates holistic education where children not only learn book knowledge but also learn practical life skills.

Chapter 80

Original Text in Simplified Characters:

ruò	liáng	hào	bā	shí	èr
若	梁	灏,	八	十	二。
duì	dà	tíng	kuí	duō	shì
对	大	廷,	魁	多	士。

Original Text in Traditional Characters:

若	梁	灝,	八	十	二。
對	大	廷,	魁	多	士。

Notes:
若: for example

対: to face

大廷: the great court

魁: to be the first, to head up

士: scholars

Modern Chinese:

宋朝有个叫梁灏的人，八十二岁高龄时，在朝廷的殿试中应答如流，战胜了所有的应试者，考上状元。

Translation:

At age eight-two, a man in the Song dynasty by the name of Liang Hao performed excellently during the oral interview in the imperial palace, and scored number one in the imperial examinations among multitudes of other scholars.

Background information:

The imperial examinations started in the Sui dynasty and ended in the Qing dynasty, lasting over 1,000 years, with a brief interruption in the Yuan dynasty during the Mongol rule. It was a system used to select local talents to join the bureaucracy in the government. The examination process was lengthy and highly competitive. The best at the local level were selected to compete at the provincial level. The national finals were interviewed by the emperor himself, although the emperor may have designated another official to examine the contestants on his behalf. The champion was called *zhuag yuan* 状元, exemplar of the State. The title came with much honor and privilege. It was the dream of every student to win the national championship and became a *zhuag yuan*.

For centuries, achieving success in the imperial examinations was a perpetual theme in almost every aspect of life in

　　　　　　　　三字經: 中華蒙學經典

梁灏八十二岁考取进士

Chinese culture. There were many stories about taking the imperial examinations. Although the examinations promoted literature, history, philosophy, and other aspects of humanities, some of the scholars were well versed in medicine and science as well. A few of the winners became exemplary statesmen. In addition to the imperial examinations in humanities, there was another imperial examination in martial arts with a similar system, where military talents were selected to join the service of the country.

Chapter 81

Original Text in Simplified Characters:

bǐ	jì	chéng	zhòng	chēng	yì
彼	既	成，	众	称	异。

ěr	xiǎo	shēng	yí	lì	zhì
尔	小	生，	宜	立	志。

Original Text in Traditional Characters:

彼	既	成，	眾	稱	異。
爾	小	生，	宜	立	志。

Notes:

成: to succeed

眾: the crowd, people

異: unusual

立志: to make resolution

Modern Chinese:

像梁灏这样老年成功的事例，大家都称颂惊奇。你们这些学子，应该像他们一样，立下志愿，努力不懈地学习。

Translation:

The case of Liang Hao who became successful at old age was truly extraordinary. Students like you should learn from his example. Set your goal, and study hard.

Background information:

Although the previous chapter noted Liang Hao was eighty-two when achieving his success, other historians set him at a much younger age. Nevertheless, any state literary champion would make a good example for any student to follow.

Chapter 82

Original Text in Simplified Characters:

yíng	bā	suì	néng	yǒng	shī
莹	八	岁，	能	咏	诗。

mì	qī	suì	néng	fù	qí
泌	七	岁，	能	赋	棋。

Original Text in Traditional Characters:

瑩	八	歲，	能	咏	詩。
泌	七	歲，	能	賦	棋。

Notes:

咏: to chant, to compose

诗: poetry

赋: to compose prose

棋: chess

Modern Chinese:

北齐时有一个叫祖莹的少年，八岁时就能作诗；唐朝时
一个叫李泌的孩子，七岁时就能按皇帝的要求当场作出
描写下围棋的好文章。

Translation:

A boy by the name of Zu Ying in the Northern Qi dynasty
was able to compose poetry at the age of eight. Another
seven-year-old boy called Li Mi in the Tang dynasty was able
to write a perfect prose essay about chess on the spot when
commanded by the emperor.

Background information:

Zu Ying was a child prodigy in the Northern Qi dynasty. Not only was he able to compose poetry at the age of eight, he was also zealous in all learning. It was said that his parents were worried about his health and forbid him to study too much. However, Zu Ying would hide fire in the ashes at night, and as soon as the servants were gone, he would light the lamp, covering the window with his blanket and clothes to read. Zu Ying became a governmental official when he grew up.

The other child prodigy, Li Mi, came from a scholar's family that had an astonishingly rich private collection of books. Once the emperor asked Li Mi to write a poem on the spot with a specified theme and style, it was a very difficult task in form and meaning. However, Li Mi produced a perfect poem to satisfy the emperor. He became the prime minister of the Tang dynasty later.

Chapter 83

Original Text in Simplified Characters:

bǐ	yǐng	wù	rén	chēng	qí
彼	颖	悟,	人	称	奇。
ěr	yòu	xué	dāng	xiào	zhī
尔	幼	学,	当	效	之。

Original Text in Traditional Characters:

彼	穎	悟,	人	稱	奇。
爾	幼	學,	當	效	之。

三字經: 中華蒙學經典

Notes:

颖悟: intelligent and perceptive

幼: young

效: to learn from, to imitate

之: them

Modern Chinese:

他们这样聪颖，大家称他们为神童。你们这些小孩子，
应该像他们学习。

Translation:

They (Zu Ying and Li Mi) were so intelligent that people
called them child prodigies. Young students such as you
should learn from them.

Background information:

Precocious children are held in high esteem in Chinese culture.
They are examples for other children to follow. Moral education, including teaching children to follow certain examples, is
another important aspect of Chinese education. As a result,
there is a tendency that children are taught to emulate others
instead of being encouraged to develop their creativity and
imagination.

Chapter 84

Original Text in Simplified Characters:

cài	wén	jī	néng	biàn	qín
蔡	文	姬,	能	辨	琴。

xiè	dào	yùn	néng	yǒng	yín
谢	道	韫,	能	咏	吟。

Original Text in Traditional Characters:

蔡	文	姬,	能	辨	琴。
謝	道	韞,	能	咏	吟。

Notes:

辨: to distinguish

琴: zither music

吟: to chant poetry

Modern Chinese:

汉朝的一个女子叫蔡文姬，她通晓音律，年少时能分辨古琴的演奏微妙之处；晋朝的才女谢道韫，自幼就擅长赋诗吟咏。

Translation:

A girl by the name Cai Wenji in the Han dynasty understood music well. As a child, she was able to decipher the minute changes in the sound of *gu qin* (Chinese zither). Another gifted girl called Xie Daoyun in the Jin dynasty was very apt in composing poetry.

Background information:

Cai Wenji was a skilled musician and scholar in Chinese history. Her father was a scholar and statesman. She knew music and literature very well. It was said that when she was six years old, she was listening to her father playing *gu qin*, the Chinese zither. A cat in the room caught a mouse, and Wenji could detect the sudden timbre on the string caused by this event. When the Huns invaded China, Cai Wenji was captured and became the wife of a tribal chief. She lived in the frontier for twelve years before returning to China, unwillingly leaving her two sons in the nomadic tribe. Cai later wrote about her life experience in an epic autobiographic poem.

Xie Daoyun was another extraordinary lady in Chinese history. She also came from a scholarly family background. Her uncle was the prime minister in the Eastern Jin dynasty. Her father-in-law was the famous calligrapher Wang Xizhi. Xie Daoyun was most well known for the vivid imagery in her poetry.

Cai Wenji

Chapter 85

Original Text in Simplified Characters:

bǐ	nǚ	zǐ	qiě	cōng	mǐn
彼	女	子,	且	聪	敏。

ěr	nán	zǐ	dāng	zì	jǐng
尔	男	子,	当	自	警。

Original Text in Traditional Characters:

彼	女	子,	且	聰	敏。
爾	男	子,	當	自	警。

Notes:

聪: clever

敏: sharp

自警: to be self alert

Modern Chinese:

她们虽然都是女子，尚且如此聪慧，你们这些男子汉，更应该自我警醒，以她们为榜样，努力学习。

Translation:

Although they were women, they were sharp and bright. You boys ought to heed their examples, learn from them, and study hard.

Background information:

Gender inequality was common in traditional Chinese culture. Women in traditional Chinese society were not allowed to receive an education. A common saying encouraged a notion that "The virtue of women resides in their ignorance. *nü zi wu cai bian shi de*, 女子无才便是德." Those who learned to read only did so when their family taught them. The audience for San Zi Jing was apparently boys. There were only three women mentioned in the entire book: Mencius' mother and these two intelligent young girls.

Chapter 86

Original Text in Simplified Characters:

táng	liú	yàn	fāng	qī	suì
唐	刘	晏，	方	七	岁。

jǔ	shén	tóng	zuò	zhèng	zì
举	神	童，	作	正	字。

Original Text in Traditional Characters:

唐	劉	晏，	方	七	歲。
舉	神	童，	作	正	字。

Notes:

举: to be chosen

神童: child prodigy

作: to be made

正字: to correct words, a title at the imperial college

Modern Chinese:

唐朝一个叫刘晏的小孩，非常聪明，才七岁时，就被推

举为神童，成为翰林书院的正字官，负责校对典籍，刊
正文字的工作。

Translation:

A boy named Liu Yan in the Tang dynasty was very bright. He was declared a child prodigy at age seven. Li Yan was given a post at the Imperial College as a corrector of texts, responsible for proofreading books and written materials.

Background information:

The Imperial College, or Royal Academy, was an institution that served as the emperor's secretarial assistant and compiled the official books on various subjects, functioning both administratively and academically. The Imperial College was initiated in the Tang dynasty, and ended at the end of the Qing dynasty. It was made up of learned scholars who passed the imperial examinations. They were considered civil servants and government officials. Liu Yan was an exceptional individual who was chosen to work in the Imperial College at a very young age.

Chapter 87

Original Text in Simplified Characters:

bǐ	suī	yòu	shēn	yǐ	shì
彼	虽	幼，	身	己	仕。
ěr	yòu	xué	miǎn	ér	zhì
尔	幼	学，	勉	而	致。
yǒu	wéi	zhě	yì	ruò	shì
有	为	者，	亦	若	是。

三字經: 中華蒙學經典

Original Text in Traditional Characters:

彼	雖	幼,	身	己	仕。
爾	幼	學,	勉	而	致。
有	為	者,	亦	若	是。

Notes:

致: to devote one's effort

有为者: those who do these

亦: also

若是: like this

Modern Chinese:

他虽然年幼，却已做官。你们这些小学生，如果从小就努力学习，也可以取得这样的成就。

Translation:

Although he (Liu Yan) was young, he became a government official. You young students should strive to study hard and concentrate on learning. If you do so, you will achieve a similar result.

Background information:

In Chinese culture, education has always been the key to career success. The goal of education is not for the sake of learning, or to "know thyself," but to become successful in finding good jobs and therefore to have a better life. Education is a stepping stone for career advancement. To endure hardship and study hard is to enjoy delayed gratification.

Chapter 88

Original Text in Simplified Characters:

quǎn	shǒu	yè	jī	sī	chén
犬	守	夜，	鸡	司	晨。

gǒu	bù	xué	hé	wéi	rén
苟	不	学，	曷	为	人。

Original Text in Traditional Characters:

犬　守　夜，　鷄　司　晨。
苟　不　學，　曷　為　人。

Notes:

犬: dog

守夜: to keep watch at night

司: to manage, serve,

苟: if

曷: how, why

为: to become

Modern Chinese:

狗会守夜，公鸡会报鸣，人如果不好好学习，怎么做人？

Translation:

Dogs bark at night for strangers or unusual activities, and roosters crow in the morning to announce the daybreak. By the same token, if a person does not apply himself in learning, how can he be a responsible person?

三字經: 中華蒙學經典

Background information:

In Chinese culture, pets are not necessary for enjoyment or personal company. They are for utilitarian purposes. The dogs are kept to protect the house and watch for strangers at night, and the roosters' crow announces the morning. The same logic holds that people are to be productive, too. Incidentally, the dog and the rooster are two of the twelve animals in the Chinese zodiac. They

are: rat, ox, tiger, rabbit, dragon, snake, horse, sheep, monkey, rooster, dog, and pig.

Chapter 89

Original Text in Simplified Characters:

chǎn	tǔ	sī	fēng	niàng	mì
蚕	吐	丝，	蜂	酿	蜜。

rén	bù	xué	bù	rú	wù
人	不	学，	不	如	物。

Original Text in Traditional Characters:

蠶	吐	絲，	蜂	釀	蜜。
人	不	學，	不	如	物。

Notes:

蚕: silk worm

吐丝: to spit silk

蜂: bee

酿蜜: to make honey

不如: not as good as

物: animals

Modern Chinese:

春蚕会吐丝供人纺织丝绸，蜜蜂会采花酿蜜供人食用。
一个人如果不学习，还不如这些小动物。

Translation:

The silkworms produce silk for people to make fabrics; the bees make honey for people to eat. If a person does not study, he is worse than animals.

Background information:

Sericulture, the technique of silk-making, was an invention of ancient China. It was a guarded trade secret for centuries, as the Chinese silk was a desired commodity in the civilized world. Raising silkworms is a delicate art. There are many factors that may contribute to the growth of the silkworm and the production and quality of the silk produced. Silkworm eggs were eventually smuggled out of China through the Silk Road, and the art of silk making was spread to Europe.

Chapter 90

Original Text in Simplified Characters:

yòu	ér	xué	zhuàng	ér	xíng
幼	而	学,	壮	而	行。

shàng	zhì	jūn	xià	zé	mín
上	致	君,	下	泽	民。

Original Text in Traditional Characters:

幼	而	學,	壯	而	行。
上	致	君,	下	澤	民。

Notes:

壯: adult

行: to carry out, to engage in

致: to extend to

君: the sovereign

泽: to nurture

民: the people

Modern Chinese:

一个人年幼的时候应当学习，到成年的时候就可以学以致用。对上能辅助君王治理国家，对下能给百姓带来益处造福人民。

Translation:

A person should study when he is young, and apply what he has learned in life when he grows up. This way, he can not only help the emperor in government service, but also benefit his countrymen.

Background information:

If a person only studies theoretical knowledge without application, it is useless. The ultimate goal for learning is to use it in life, and more importantly, use the knowledge for the benefit of the country. Therefore, to study hard is also a patriotic act. It is indeed a very worthy and noble endeavor.

Chapter 91

Original Text in Simplified Characters:

yáng	míng	shēng	xiǎn	fù	mǔ
扬	名	声，	显	父	母。
guāng	yú	qián	yù	yú	hòu
光	于	前，	裕	于	后。

Original Text in Traditional Characters:

揚　名　聲，　顯　父　母。
光　于　前，　裕　于　后。

Notes:

显: to make noticeable

光: to glorify

前: ancestors

裕: to make abundant

后: offspring, descendents

Modern Chinese:

学习和人生的目的是为了争取好的名声，荣耀父母。一个人应该既为祖先前辈争光，又给子孙后代留下财富。

Translation:

The purpose of learning in life is to have a reputable name and to honor one's parents. One should strive to bring glory to his ancestors, and richness and prosperity to his descendents.

Background information:

Filial piety is an essential element in Chinese culture. It requires people to respect, obey, and bring honor to their elders. Filial piety is a central tenant in Confucianism. Children are taught at a young age to listen to, obey, and bring honor to their parents and ancestors. Another important aspect of filial piety requires an individual to perpetuate the family line. Chinese parents often devote their lives for their children and grandchildren's wellbeing.

Chapter 92

Original Text in Simplified Characters:

rén	yí	zǐ	jīn	mǎn	yíng
人	遗	子,	金	满	赢。

wǒ	jiào	zǐ	wéi	yì	jīng
我	教	子,	惟	一	经。

Original Text in Traditional Characters:

人	遺	子,	金	滿	贏。
我	教	子,	惟	一	經。

Notes:

遗: to give, to bequeath

满: full

赢: chest

惟: only

Modern Chinese:

别人留给子孙的是满箱的金银财宝，而我给子弟留下的只是对他们的教育，只给他们留下这样一部三字经，让他们好好念诵，学习做人处事的道理。

Translation:

While some people leave their descendents chests of gold and treasure, I only have my students inherit the teachings through the book of San Zi Jing, the *Three Character Classic,* so that they may recite the text and learn the proper ways of life.

Background information:

A popular Chinese saying notes that "Wealth does not last longer than three generations. *fu bu chuan san dai* 富不传三代." In traditional Chinese society, it is rare for a family to pass  their wealth and property to multiple generations. While it is common for extended family to live together, with grandfather, father, and the sons' family, the extended family normally dissolves when the father dies and the property was shared among the brothers. Sometimes brothers became arch enemies because of conflict arising in inheritance.

Another Chinese proverb says, "It is better to read and understand the classics than to accumulate tangible wealth." *ji jin wan liang, bu ru shu du jing shu* 积金万两，不如熟读经书. Education has always been considered very important.

Chapter 93

Original Text in Simplified Characters:

qín	yǒu	gōng	xì	wú	yì
勤	有	功,	戏	无	益。

jiè	zhī	zāi	yí	miǎn	lì
戒	之	哉,	宜	勉	力。

Original Text in Traditional Characters:

勤　有　功，　戲　無　益。
戒　之　哉，　宜　勉　力。

Notes:

有功: to have merit

戏: play

无益: no benefit, unprofitable

戒: to guard

哉: oh

勉力: to exert strength, to strive hard

Modern Chinese:

勤奋一定会有功效，不认真学习嬉戏游玩，没有益处。
请一定注意，自我警醒，时时勉励自己，努力学习。

Translation:

Hard work will bring success; play and negligence of learning will result in no benefit. Please be warned and avoid idleness. Be diligent at all times, and do strive to study hard.

Background information:

Diligence and hard work will result in success, and play is fruitless. Studying is like sailing against the tide, if one does not go forward, he will go backward inevitably. Students need to make progress at all times. Time is a non-renewable resource. A minute is like a gold nugget, but a gold nugget cannot buy a minute. *yi cun guang yin yi cun jin, cun jin nan mai cun guang yin* 一寸光阴一寸金，寸金难买寸光阴. While the students are young, it is of utmost importance for them to use their time wisely and study hard.

A Brief Chronology of Chinese History

Xia Dynasty			2070-1600 BCE
Shang Dynasty			1600-1046 BCE
Zhou Dynasty		Western Zhou	1046-771 BCE
		Eastern Zhou	770-256 BCE
		Spring & Autumn Period	770-476 BCE
		Warring States Period	475-221 BCE
Qin Dynasty			221-206 BCE
Han Dynasty		Western Han	206 BCE-25 CE
		Eastern Han	25-220
Three Kingdoms		Wei	220-265
		Shu Han	221-263
		Wu	222-280
Western Jin Dynasty			265-317
Eastern Jin Dynasty			317-420
Northern and Southern Dynasties	Southern Dynasties	Song	420-479
		Qi	479-502
		Liang	502-557
		Chen	557-589
	Northern Dynasties	Northern Wei	386-534
		Eastern Wei	534-550
		Northern Qi	550-577
		Western Wei	535-556
		Northern Zhou	557-581
Sui Dynasty			581-618

三字經: 中華蒙學經典

Tang Dynasty		618-907
Five Dynasties	Later Liang	907-923
	Later Tang	923-936
	Later Jin	936-947
	Later Han	947-950
	Later Zhou	951-960
Song Dynasty	Northern Song	960-1127
	Southern Song	1127-1279
Liao Dynasty		907-1125
Jin Dynasty		1115-1234
Yuan Dynasty		1206-1368
Ming Dynasty		1368-1644
Qing Dynasty		1644-1911

Selected Bibliography

Bischoff, Friedrich Alexander. *San tzu ching explicated: the classical initiation to classic Chinese couplet I to XI.* Beiträge zur Kultur- und Geistesgeschichte Asiens; Nr. 45. Wien: Verlag der Österreichischen Akademie der Wissenschaften, 2005.

Giles, H.A. *The san tzu ching: or three character classic, and the ch'ien tsu wên, or thousand character essay.* Translated by Herbert A. Giles. Shanghai: A. H. de Carvalho, 1873.

————. *Elementary Chinese: san tzu ching.* Translated and annotated by Herbert A. Giles. Shanghai: Kelly & Walsh, 1900.

————. *Elementary Chinese: san tzu ching.* 2nd ed., rev. Translated and annotated by Herbert A. Giles. Shanghai: Kelly & Walsh, 1910.

————. *San tzu ching: Elementary Chinese.* 2nd ed., rev. Translated and annotated by Herbert A. Giles. New York: Ungar, 1963.

————. *San tzu ching: Elementary Chinese.* 2nd ed., rev. Translated and annotated by Herbert A. Giles. Taipei, Taiwan: Literature House, 1964.

Legge, James. *The Chinese classics: with a translation, critical and exegetical notes, prolegomena, and copious indexes.* 5 Volumes. Taipei: Southern Materials Center, 1985.

Mao, Zengyin. *Verses in three characters and genre pictures.* Beijing: Wu Zhou Chuan Bo Publishing House, 2005.

Morrison, Robert. *Horæ sinicæ: translations from the popular literature of the Chinese.* Includes San tzu ching, Da xue and Extract from

三字經: 中華蒙學經典

the Ho-kiang. Translation by Robert Morrison. London: Printed for Black and Parry by C. Stower, 1812.

Phen, S. T. *San tzu ching. English & Chinese.* Translated by S. T. Phen, illustrated by Ng, Edwn & Zhou, Songsheng. Singapore: EPB Publishers, 1989.

————. *San tzu ching. English & Chinese. Three character classic in pictures.* Translated by S. T. Phen; edited by Xu Chuiyang; illustrated by Sheng Liangxian. Singapore: EPB Publishers, 1990.

Acknowledgements

During the course of researching and translating San Zi Jing, I have sought and received help from many. I would like to thank the Faculty Summer Research Committee at Lee University, chaired by Dr. Ollie Lee, for funding me a trip to view the rare books and do research on this project at Harvard University.

I would like to thank the librarian at Harvard Yenching Library, especially Ms. Sharon Li-Shiuan Yang and her staff. Their assistance made my research at the library most efficient. I would like to thank Mr. Chun Shum of the Harvard Yenching Library Rare Books Collection for giving me permission to take photos of the San Zi Jing rare books.

I would like to thank Ms. Barbara McCullough at the Squares Library at Lee University and her staff, Ms. Diette Ward at the interlibrary loan service and Mr. Frank Shroyer at the circulation desk, for fulfilling my numerous requests for borrowing materials and interlibrary loans.

I thank Jian Zheng for reading my Chinese manuscript and taking time to type the Chinese characters. I also thank Edward Goodman for assisting me in many aspects of the research.

My husband, Randy Gray, gave me wise input and valuable support through my writing and thinking process.

Professor Fan Yuzhou at Nanjing University edited the Chinese translation. He gave me much guidance on interpreting classic Chinese. I feel very fortunate to have such an expert critique the Chinese translation. Professor Fan also kindly wrote the Chinese introduction to this book.

My colleague Dr. Christopher Coulter, Associate Professor of English, loaned me his expertise on editing the entire English manuscript, for which I am deeply grateful. I also thank my colleague Dr. Arden Jensen for proof-reading the sample chapters and gave me valuable advice. In addition, I thank Dr. Jean Eledge and my dear friend Mr. Norman Ziggrossi for their wise and kind encouragement.

I am thankful to my publisher, Mr. Shawn Ye, for giving me the opportunity to share this classic Chinese work with contemporary readers. I am most grateful to Mr. Ye for his excellent suggestion on shaping the book the way it is.

I consulted the following previous San Zi Jing authors' work as my main references: H.A. Giles (1845-1935); Wang Xiang 王相 and He Xingsi 贺兴思 of the Qing dynasty, and Zhang Taiyan 章太炎. I also referenced a modern translation by Professor Louis Smoger at Depauw University, who generously shared with me his experiences with San Zi Jing. I came to admire H.A. Giles, a pioneering sinologist, for his understanding of San Zi Jing, and from here I started to reach on his life and work.

Even though I have labored much on this project, it is by no means perfect. I will take credit for any error.

Phebe X. Gray

Homa & Sekey Books Titles on China

Managing China's Modernization: Perspectives on Diplomacy, Politics, Education and Ethnicity by Dr. Edwin Pak-wah Leung. Order No. 1078, ISBN: 9781931907743, Hardcover, xvi, 338p, $59.95, History/Politics

The Three Character Classic: A Bilingual Reader of China's ABCs by Dr. Phebe Xu Gray. Order No. 1075, ISBN: 9781931907712, Paperback, xx, 191p, $19.95, Language/Culture

China's Terracotta Army and the First Emperor's Mausoleum by Yuan Zhongyi. Order No. 1072, ISBN: 9781931907682, Paperback, 152p, Color illustrations throughout, $29.95, Culture/History/Art

THE LEGEND OF HAIBAO SERIES
(Paperback, All color, Cartoon/Comics)
The Legend of Haibao 1: The Myth of the Crystal Palace, Order No. 1067, ISBN: 9781931907637, 96p, $14.95
The Legend of Haibao 2: A Journey of the Gourmet, Order No. 1068, ISBN: 9781931907644, 96p, $14.95
The Legend of Haibao 3: Meeting Friends from Afar, Order No. 1069, ISBN: 9781931907651, 96p, $14.95
The Legend of Haibao 4: A Journey through Space, Order No. 1070, ISBN: 9781931907668, 96p, $14.95

Folk Culture in China's Zhejiang Province: The Flowing Mother River by Tong Shaosu, trans. by Yu Jianqing and Shen Mingxia. Order No. 1066, ISBN: 9781931907620, Paperback, 216p, Color illustrations throughout, $29.95, Culture/History

The History of Chinese Printing by Zhang Xiumin, revised by Dr. Han Qi, trans. by Chen Jiehua et al. Order No. 1065, ISBN: 9781931907613, Paperback, 550p, Color illustrations throughout, Limited edition, History

EDUCATION IN CHINA SERIES (Hardcover)
Educational System in China by Ming Yang. Order No. 1060, ISBN: 9781931907569, 410p
Educational Policies and Legislation in China by Xiaozhou Xu et al. Order No. 1061, ISBN: 9781931907576, 275p

Basic Education in China by Libing Wang. Order No. 1062, ISBN: 9781931907583, 147p

Higher Education in China by Jianmin Gu et al. Order No. 1063, ISBN: 9781931907590, 227p

Technical and Vocational Education in China by Xueping Wu et al. Order No. 1064, ISBN: 9781931907606, 283p

Seven Kinds of Mushrooms: A Novel of the Cultural Revolution by Zhang Wei, trans. by Terence Russell. Order No. 1059, ISBN: 9781931907552, Paperback, 214p, $16.95, Fiction

Two Lifetimes: A Novel by Joanne Guo. Order No. 1058, ISBN: 9781931907545, Paperback, 242p, $16.95, Fiction

The Art of Mogao Grottoes in Dunhuang: A Journey into China's Buddhist Shrine by Fan Jinshi & Zhao Shengliang. Order No. 1057, ISBN: 9781931907538, Paperback, 172p, Color illustrations throughout, $29.95, Art, Buddhism

Everything I Understand About America I Learned in Chinese Proverbs by Wendy Liu. Order No. 1056, ISBN: 9781931907521, Paperback, 173p, $16.95, Social Studies

The Chopsticks-Fork Principle x2: A Bilingual Reader by Cathy Bao Bean and Dongdong Chen. Order No. 1055, ISBN: 9781931907514, Paperback, xx, 328p, $59.95, Language/Culture

From Ironing Board to Corporate Board: My Chinese Laundry Experience in America by Ginny Gong. Order No. 1054, ISBN: 9781931907507, Paperback, 151p, $12.95, Asian-American

September's Fable: A Novel by Zhang Wei, trans. by Terrence Russell & Shawn X. Ye. Order No. 1050, ISBN: 9781931907460, Paperback, 495p, $29.95, Fiction

The Bitter Sea: "Morphing" and Other Stories by David Ke, PhD. Order No. 1048, ISBN: 9781931907446, Paperback, 226p, $16.95, Fiction/Asian Studies

Journey across the Four Seas: A Chinese Woman's Search for Home by Veronica Li. Order No. 1047, ISBN: 9781931907439, Paperback, 298p, with b&w photo inserts, $14.95, Nonfiction/Memoir

The Holy Spark: Rogel and the Goddess of Liberty by Yu Li. Order No. 1046, ISBN 9781931907422, Hardcover, 260p, b&w illustrations throughout, $16.99, Fiction/Children

Willow Leaf, Maple Leaf: A Novel of Immigration Blues by David Ke, PhD. Order No. 1036, ISBN: 9781931907248, Paperback, 203p, $16.95, Fiction/Asian-American Studies

China's Generation Y: Understanding the Future Leaders of the World's Next Superpower (with b&w photo inserts) by Michael Stanat, United Nations International School.
Order No. 1029, ISBN 9781931907255, Hardcover, 222p, $24.95;
Order No. 1040, ISBN 9781931907323, Paperback, 222p, $17.95,
Contemporary Affairs

Paintings by Xu Jin: Tradition and Innovation in Chinese Fine Brushwork, foreword by Prof. Robert E. Harrist, Jr., Columbia University. Order No. 1028, ISBN 9781931907231, Hardcover, 128p, Color illustrations throughout, $39.50, Art

The Eleventh Son: A Novel of Martial Arts and Tangled Love by Gu Long, trans. by Rebecca S. Tai. Order No. 1020, ISBN: 9781931907163, Paperback, 320p, $19.95, Fiction/Martial Arts

Breaking Grounds: The Journal of a Top Chinese Woman Manager in Retail by Bingxin Hu, Foreword by Louis B. Barnes, Harvard Business School. Order No. 1019, ISBN: 9781931907156, Hardcover, 256p, with b&w photo inserts, $24.95, Business

The Dream of the Red Chamber: An Allegory of Love by Jeannie Jinsheng Yi, PhD.
Order No. 1016, ISBN: 9780966542172, Hardcover, b&w illustrations throughout, $49.95, Asian Studies/Literary Criticism

The Haier Way: The Making of a Chinese Business Leader and a Global Brand by Jeannie J. Yi, PhD & Shawn X. Ye, MBA. Order No. 1009, ISBN: 9781931907019, Hardcover, 280p, with b&w photo inserts, $24.95, Business

Splendor of Tibet: The Potala Palace, Jewel of the Himalayas by Phuntsok Namgyal. Order No. 1008, ISBN: 9781931907026, Hardcover, 160p, $39.95, Art/Architecture

Ink Paintings by Gao Xingjian, the Nobel Prize Winner
Order No. 1007, ISBN: 9781931907033, Hardcover, 92p,
$34.95, Art

Musical Qigong: Ancient Chinese Healing Art from a Modern Master by Shen Wu. Order No. 1006, ISBN: 9780966542158,
Paperback, 160p, b&w photo and illustrations throughout, $14.95,
Body-Mind, Self-help

Always Bright, Vol. II: Paintings by Chinese American Artists
edited by Eugene Wang, Harvard Univ., et al. Order No. 1005, ISBN:
9780966542165, Hardcover, 208p, $50.00, Art

Always Bright: Paintings by American Chinese Artists 1970-1999
edited by Xue Jian Xin et al. Order No. 1004,
ISBN: 9780966542134, Hardcover, 180p, $49.95, Art

Butterfly Lovers: A Tale of the Chinese Romeo and Juliet
by Fan Dai, PhD. Order No. 1003, ISBN: 9780966542141, Paperback,
256p, $16.95, Fiction

The Peony Pavilion: A Novel by Xiaoping Yen, PhD.
Order No. 1002, ISBN: 9780966542127, Paperback, 256p, $16.95,
Fiction

Flower Terror: Suffocating Stories of China by Pu Ning, trans.
by Richard Ferris, Jr. & Andrew Morton. Order No. 1001, ISBN:
9780966542103, Paperback, 256p, $13.95, Fiction

www.homabooks.com

Ordering Information: Within U.S.: $5.00 for the first item, $1.50 for each additional
item. **Outside U.S.:** $14.00 for the first item, $7.00 for each additional item. All major credit
cards accepted. You may also send a check or money order in U.S. fund (payable to Homa
& Sekey Books) to: Orders Department, Homa & Sekey Books, P. O. Box 103, Dumont,
NJ 07628 U.S.A. Tel: 800-870-HOMA, 201-261-8810; Fax: 201-261-8890, 201-384-6055;
Email: info@homabooks.com.

CPSIA information can be obtained at www.ICGtesting.com
Printed in the USA
LVOW06s1848151115

462668LV00029B/1347/P